The Hidden Curriculum of Getting and Keeping a Job

The Hidden Curriculum of Getting and Keeping a Job: Navigating the Social Landscape of Employment

A Guide for Individuals With Autism Spectrum and Other Social-Cognitive Challenges

**Brenda Smith Myles, PhD,
Judy Endow, MSW,
and Malcolm Mayfield, BS Civil Eng**

FUTURE HORIZONS

www.fhautism.com

info@fhautism.com

817.277.0727

Publisher's Cataloging-in-Publication

Myles, Brenda Smith.

The hidden curriculum of getting and keeping a job : navigating the social landscape of employment : a guide for individuals with autism spectrum and other social-cognitive challenges / Brenda Smith Myles, Judy Endow, and Malcolm Mayfield.

p. ; cm.

ISBN: 978-1-937473-02-0
LCCN: 2012948937
Includes bibliographical references.
Summary: The hidden curriculum, those unspoken rules that most of us pick up almost unconsciously, are challenging for individuals with autism and similar social-cognitive disorders. This book offers easy, simple to follow suggestions for how to avoid the social minefields in getting and keeping a job.
1. Autistic people--Life skills guides. 2. Autistic people--Employment. 3. Cognition disorders--Patients--Life skills guides. 4. Cognition disorders--Patients--Employment. 5. Autism spectrum disorders--Patients--Life skills guides. 6. Autism spectrum disorders--Patients--Employment. 7. Social skills--Study and teaching. 8. Social learning--Study and teaching. I. Endow, Judy. II. Mayfield, Malcolm. III. Title. IV. Title: Navigating the social landscape of employment.

1210

Table of Contents

Chapter One:

What Is the Hidden Curriculum?

■ ■ ■

ABC Inc. announced via email to its employees that it was holding its annual company picnic at Filmore Park. The email stated that the event was casual and to come prepared for fun and games.

This was Mark's first company picnic. He had been with ABC for almost one year and enjoyed his work as a technology assistant. His autism had been both an asset and a challenge at work. Mark prepared carefully for the picnic. He packed his favorite games (Scrabble, Trivial Pursuit, Risk, Angry Birds, Parcheesi, and Dungeons and Dragons 4E Caves of Chaos) into two boxes. He also brought a picnic basket filled with peanut butter sandwiches and Gatorade. When Mark arrived at the picnic, he was surprised when a fellow employee pulled him aside and said, "You messed up, dude!" The games were not board games, and the entire affair was catered.

■ ■ ■

The hidden curriculum is the set of assumed knowledge that is generally not directly taught because it is considered to be universally known and understood. Its content is typically reflected in expectations, guidelines, attitudes, values, beliefs, terminology, behavior, and other messages that are conveyed indirectly through inferences and assumptions (Cornbleth, 2011; Jackson, 1968; Kanpol, 1989; LaVoie 1994; Myles, Trautman, & Schelvan, 2013). It is also often called common sense.

Because this information is not directly conveyed, it can pose a minefield of unexpected reactions and behaviors for those, like Mark, to whom it is not innate or by whom it is not easily picked up from their environment. Understanding and adhering to the unwritten rules and expectations of the hidden curriculum is important throughout life, but for adults it is especially critical in the workplace. This means self-evaluating, observing others, solving problems, making decisions, and seeking assistance, as needed (Landmark, Ju, & Zhang, 2010; Wehmeyer, Gragoudas, & Shogren, 2006). For example, if all of your fellow employees take a notepad into the weekly meeting, good observational skills or asking around would help you to realize that it is essential to bring a notepad or some type of recording device and that notes are expected to be taken during the meeting.

The hidden curriculum includes the different ways that skills are executed across a range of individuals, situations, and environments. Learning the hidden curriculum will help those who do not detect the subtleties of situations and who tend to be routine bound, literal, and rule enforcers.

Mark in the example above did not understand the hidden curriculum of company picnics. Company picnics have a specific set of expectations that are often not communicated. These include:

- Unless otherwise specified, the company provides the food. Employees know to bring food if they are asked to bring a specific item or to sign up to bring something. It is then each person's responsibility to bring his or her item. It is appropriate to ask how much to bring.
- If you have dietary restrictions, it is appropriate to bring a serving of your own food to eat at the event or you may choose to

eat beforehand. Some company invitations ask if any attendees have an allergy or other dietary restriction. If so, it is appropriate to inform the contact person about the food category you cannot eat. It is not necessary to indicate how the particular food impacts your body.

- Unless otherwise specified, don't bring games and activities to a company picnic.
- There is generally a dress code for picnics. If you are unsure, ask a trusted colleague what he is wearing to the event.
- There is generally a beginning and an ending time for company picnics. Unless you are in charge of setting up the picnic, it is best not to arrive early. Also, it is not advisable to be the last one to leave.
- During the event, it is appropriate to thank your boss for hosting the picnic. When doing so, unless the boss wants to talk with you about business, talk about other topics such as current TV shows, sports, etc.

The Hidden Curriculum Rules Go Beyond the Employee Handbook

The example of Mark also illustrates incongruities in terminology, another aspect of the hidden curriculum. That is, words and phrases often have different meanings across environments, activities, and individuals. Mark understood that he was supposed to "come prepared for fun and games." In his mind, this meant that he was to bring games that he considered fun. He did not understand that this statement merely meant that the picnic was supposed to be enjoyable.

This book addresses the hidden curriculum as it unfolds throughout the process of entering and participating in the workforce. The hidden curriculum impacts all areas of employment, social interactions, work performance, promotions, and safety. It can even determine whether or not a person is hired for a job.

Despite its considerable value, however, information about the hidden curriculum often remains truly "hidden" to the unsuspecting "victim" until a social blunder occurs. And what makes it confusing and frustrating is that the hidden curriculum rules cannot be found in the employee handbook, for example, because they are considered "common knowledge."

■ ■ ■

Maritha had read the employee manual carefully and memorized all aspects that she felt applied to her. She specifically noted that personal calls were not to be made during work hours. She was indignant when she received a written warning for texting her boyfriend at work because this was not specifically covered in the manual. When Maritha pointed this out to her supervisor, he thought she was being rude, which resulted in a tenuous work relationship between the two.

After several similar incidents, Maritha was fired six months later for taking two rolls of toilet paper home because she didn't have time to go to the grocery store to buy some. When confronted by that same supervisor, Maritha directed him to the employee handbook, which referred only to not taking office supplies home. She told him, "Clearly, toilet paper is NOT office supplies." A recent evaluation revealed that her work performance was "excellent."

■ ■ ■

Hidden curriculum items related to Maritha's situation ...

- Activities that take away from work time, such as making personal phone calls, sending personal emails, and texting should be minimal. Ask a supervisor about the company's policy concerning this.
- It is a good idea not to take any items for personal use from work. This is considered theft.

Violating the Hidden Curriculum Can Have a Variety of Consequences, Some of Them Very Serious

While individual errors may be inconsequential, some are more noticeable and more serious than others. As in the example of Maritha, these errors in the workplace often result in reprimands and even termination.

The hidden curriculum also encompasses behaviors of such a serious nature that they are illegal. Even though specific actions are against the law, they are often not included in typical instructions, nor are they explained in enough detail to be helpful for literal learners, who have difficulty generalizing information. A case in point is sexual harassment, as illustrated in the following.

■ ■ ■

Khan ended up with serious problems because he didn't understand that his daily compliments to a female coworker were considered sexual harassment. Each day, he gave this coworker what he considered very nice compliments, such as "You have very pretty legs" or "You look hot when your shirts are tight."

Eventually, the coworker reported the situation to her boss. When questioned afterward, Khan not only admitted that he made these (and similar) comments but defended himself by saying that because his comments were truthful, there wasn't anything wrong with them. After all, he had often been told that telling the truth would not get you into trouble.

Khan was told to stop making these types of comments. He did, but unwittingly he substituted comments that were even worse. Once again, he thought he was following the rules because he did stop saying the comments his boss specifically told him to stop saying by substituting new truths. Ultimately, he was fired for telling the female coworker, "I wish I was your boyfriend so I could have sex with you."

■ ■ ■

Hidden curriculum item related to Khan's situation ...

- Sexual harassment is against the law. It is defined as *unwelcome verbal, visual, or physical conduct of a sexual nature.* If you wish to pay someone a compliment, it must be a general comment, such as "You look very nice today." And to be considered sincere, compliments should not be given often.

Understanding the Hidden Curriculum Can Help Solve Workplace Problems

The hidden curriculum also includes knowing how to solve problems in the workplace. Generally, there are hidden curriculum rules for (a) whom to seek assistance from and (b) when to seek it; often this is associated with the *chain of command.* This term refers to the order in which authority is exercised from company management down to hourly employees. Some employees don't understand their employer's chain of command or when they are to adhere to it, as illustrated in the case of Sandy.

■ ■ ■

Sandy submitted the appropriate paperwork to the accounting department for reimbursement for a work-related conference she had attended. From talking with other employees, she knew that she could expect to receive a check in approximately two weeks.

Two weeks passed without a check being issued. Instead of talking directly to the accounting supervisor, Sandy told several of her colleagues that she had not been reimbursed. She even expressed her concern on the company's Facebook page as well as on her personal Facebook page. In addition, she advised coworkers not to attend an upcoming conference because they, too, would likely not be reimbursed for their expenses. After each recounting of the story, Sandy became more upset.

A coworker in the accounting department attempted to resolve the issue on her behalf. Only then was it was discovered that Sandy's invoice had accidentally been routed to the wrong person. When this error was detected, the accounting manager met with Sandy to apologize and give her the check. But by this time, Sandy was so upset that she called the accounting manager a liar and continued to spread misinformation.

■ ■ ■

Hidden curriculum item related to Sandy's situation ...

- If a problem occurs at work, discuss it with your supervisor. Many problems are simply mistakes that can be corrected as soon as they are brought to the attention of a supervisor.

It Is All About the Context

Many hidden curriculum errors occur when a correlation is lacking among (a) who is involved in the situation; (b) the setting, environment, or activity; and (c) the timing of the situation. Thinking about how factors correlate helps when attempting to generalize information regarding the hidden curriculum, as illustrated in Figure 1.1. Peter Vermeulen (2012) refers to this as context blindness.

Figure 1.1. **Hidden curriculum considerations.**

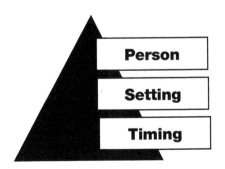

Person

It may be helpful to think of the company's chain of command or organizational chart when considering the "who" in the workplace. As shown in Figure 1.2, Chou is the direct supervisor for Reaux, Bell, and Mourna. Watkins is the head of the division or organization, and Chou reports directly to her. Watkins, Chou, and Bell have administrative assistants. Generally, less formal language can be used with others at the same level of the organizational chart (with Reaux, Bell, and Mourna) than with someone "higher up" on the chain of command or individuals outside of the organization.

Figure 1.2. Sample organizational chart.

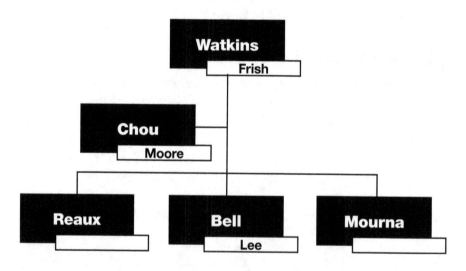

For example, an employee can greet a colleague by saying, "Whass up?" when they are alone or with fellow employees in a relaxed setting, such as break or lunch. However, the same greeting should not be used in front of a boss or client, or at a meeting, where a more formal statement would be appropriate.

If advice is needed on how to complete a project, it is generally best to ask the person who assigned the task. So in this case, Bell would ask Chou. If administrative support is needed, it is appropriate to ask the administrative assistant assigned to you or the project; it is generally not acceptable to ask an assistant who reports directly to someone else. As a general rule, do not to engage in gossip about those with whom you work, no matter where they are located on the chain of command.

Setting

Somewhat formal and work-related communication should occur in designated work environments, such as offices, cubicles, or meeting rooms. It is typically acceptable to share very brief communications of a somewhat personal nature when first entering a work area, such as "How was your weekend" on a Monday or Tuesday, or by making reference to a particular event that you knew that someone was looking forward to, as this type of communication is a preamble to work-related conversation. Conversation in the lunch or break room is generally informal in nature, and is devoted to mutual interests outside of work, activities that may be of interest to others, and similar topics. Conversation in company outings and events, such as birthday celebrations, are almost always devoted to nonwork-related topics of conversation. When in doubt, observe the behavior of others to determine what to do.

Timing

Olympian Carl Lewis (http://www.brainyquote.com/quotes/quotes/c/carllewis126092.html) says that life is about timing. Timing has to do with a variety of factors, such as ascertaining others' mood. If an employee wishes to ask for a favor, a raise, a day off, and so forth, she should make sure that the person she is asking is in a good mood and has time to listen. Making a request of someone who is angry, in a meeting with someone else, engaged in a deep conversation, or rushing out of the office generally does not lead to a positive outcome. Considering the time of day is also important. Beginning a conversation that will require more than a few seconds of discussion five minutes before work ends, or right before lunch or a meeting, is generally not a good idea.

Summary

The hidden curriculum – the unspoken rules, expectations, and guidelines for social interactions – impacts every aspect of the work environment. Although it may not directly relate to the caliber of your job performance, understanding and adhering to the hidden curriculum can affect whether or not you maintain your position. Careful instruction, on-the-job-support, and learning to use strong observational skills are all tools needed to learn and understand the hidden curriculum.

Chapter Two

Finding a Job

In the quest for employment, the act of finding a job opening is the easy part. The challenge lies in preparing for that job, pursuing it, and then securing it. We become the hunter when looking for work. In our mind, we have a well-defined image of the prey or job that we seek. What we lack to varying degrees is the knowledge of how to hunt that prey and what to do with it if we are successful.

Being prepared is critical for gaining employment. This includes ...

- Identifying the skills and experiences required for employment;
- Researching the skills and experiences that employers are looking for in an employee;
- Implementing strategies to acquire skills and experience. This may include using mentors, employment agencies, and training organizations; and
- Compiling a resume and gathering references that will give you the greatest success in getting the attention of prospective employers.

This chapter will guide you through the following aspects of preparing for and then getting a job: mentoring; employment agencies; Vocational Rehabilitation; networking; social media; using your natural resources; and creating a resume.

The Role of Mentors

Dictionary.com defines "mentor" as "a wise and trusted counselor or teacher" and "an influential senior sponsor or supporter." "Mentoring," therefore, can be described as the act of transferring wisdom.

When it comes to finding a job, having a mentor can be crucial. Depending on the situation, anyone can be a mentor. Throughout our lives we will have many and varied mentors, starting with our parents and family. Teachers, friends, even enemies, people we meet only once, and also fictional characters in television, movies, and books can all be mentors. The key is to find someone who can guide us to success. This can and often will be more than one person.

In fact, mentoring does not always involve a live human being. The act of reading a book on finding a job can create a mentoring relationship between the reader and the author. This book is itself a mentor on your journey.

There are mentors available for most activities in life, and especially for finding and maintaining employment. As with any search, the best starting point is with familiar territory – your family, friends, and those with whom you have a caring relationship. Such people can mentor you through your first steps into employment, giving encouragement and guidance, and maybe even access to more experienced mentors. Mentors are an excellent resource for learning the hidden curriculum.

Employment agencies are also good sources for finding mentors. Organizations that are specifically tailored to your needs and skills often provide experienced mentors who assist you with both your job preparedness and job searching according to your special requirements.

Be open to mentoring in any form from any credible source, and you will likely be surprised at just how many mentors will be available to assist you in your journey through life.

■ ■ ■

Kim is a vibrant, talented individual with a high self-awareness and openness toward his strengths and needs. Upon completion of his postgraduate studies in civil engineering, Kim sought the advice of his father's friend, Joanne, who attends their place of worship. She is an engineer for a mid-sized company. Joanne agreed to be Kim's mentor. She and Kim subsequently developed an agreement that specified the details of their mentor-mentee relationship.

Joanne quickly determined that Kim's openness about and awareness of his autism as well as his engineering knowledge were assets and, with Kim's consent, she wrote a cover letter to prospective employers from her perspective of him, openly explaining Kim's diagnosis. The goal was to find an employer who was already aware of autism or who was willing to learn about it and to make suitable adjustments for Kim in the workplace.

Kim applied to many organizations, receiving few responses, mainly because his field of expertise was very competitive. Then Joanne became aware of a paid postgraduate position within an organization renowned for diversity and for employing people with disabilities. She had met a representative from this company at an industry event and forwarded Kim's letter to him. The application elicited a quick response from the firm's human resources manager, who expressed an active interest in learning more about Kim's autism.

Joanne prepared Kim for an interview. The interview went well, and Kim was called in for a second interview and, ultimately, secured the position over 100 other applicants!

Joanne accompanied Kim to work on his first day to ensure that he was oriented to his new surroundings. She phased out her support as the firm's internal mentoring program, specifically tailored for people with autism, took effect. Joanne still offers phone support to Kim whenever he needs it and occasionally visits his workplace to see how he is doing. She also offers ongoing support and advice to Kim's line manager. Kim is still employed by this organization and is very happy working there.

■ ■ ■

Hidden curriculum items related to Kim's situation ...

• Choose a mentor who has experience in the profession you are seeking. Consider these traits in a mentor: (a) success in doing the work required by the profession, (b) savvy about how to interact with people in the workplace, (c) time to engage in mentoring, and (d) a straightforward communicator.

• Establish the guidelines for the mentoring relationship by developing a written mentoring agreement with the mentor. A good mentoring agreement contains the following components: (a) names of mentee and mentor(s), (b) length of agreement; (c) mentoring objectives, (d) assistance to be provided by mentor, (e) responsibilities to be assumed by the mentee, (f) how learning outcomes will be measured, (g) how and when communication will occur as well as other communication parameters, such as length and/or frequency of contact, (h) confidentiality, (i) boundaries and topics to avoid, and (j) how to resolve conflicts. This will ensure that there will be fewer mistakes in the mentoring process, such as contacting the mentor too often or at the wrong time.

Sample mentoring agreements may be found at:

  – http://www.coachingandmentoring.com/Mentor/contract.htm

  – www.beamentor.org/coordfrms/Our%20Mentoring%20 Agreement.rtf

  – http://www.educause.edu/Mentoring+Home/FortheMentor/ MentoringAgreement/206375

  – http://hrdailyadvisor.blr.com/archive/2009/07/30/Training_ Mentoring_Agreement_Contract.aspx.

Hidden curriculum items related to Kim's situation ...

- It is okay to have several mentors. In fact, it is encouraged. The more sources you can draw wisdom from, the better skilled you will be for achieving your goals.

- Characters in books, television shows, movies, and other media can be mentors as they are drawn from the experiences of those who created them. However, if you are going to use such a character as a mentor, you must be able and willing to distinguish his or her illusionary situation from your real-world needs.

- Keep in mind that the mentor is there to guide you professionally. Her interest in helping you should not be construed as romantic or as a friendship. To believe that this person is anything other than a mentor may lead to her becoming uncomfortable and terminating the mentoring agreement. *This is a professional relationship.* Even though the relationship is professional, you may receive mentoring on personal topics, such as hygiene, making small talk, and so forth, because these issues will likely impact you on the job.

- You are not contracted to believe everything that the mentor tells you. Neither are you contracted to do everything that she suggests. Your role is to listen, investigate the validity of what you are told as it relates to your situation, and adopt it if it works for you.

- There are no guarantees that the mentor will help you to achieve your goal. Ultimately, your success depends upon your own actions. The mentor is merely there to help you develop better skills for achieving success.

- It is okay to be confused about the information you are receiving from the mentor. Confusion gives you an opportunity to find out why you are confused and how you can reorganize the information so that you can better understand it. Your mentor can help you with this process. Ask questions if you are confused. Even if you think that you understand your mentor, it is often wise to paraphrase back the information or provide an example of how it can be used.

Hidden curriculum items related to Kim's situation ...

- The mentoring agreement should include a "no fault" provision for ending the mentoring relationship. If you enter into negativity or blaming at the termination of the agreement, you may block future avenues of mentoring.
- You have as much right as the mentor to end the mentoring relationship.
- Ending the mentoring relationship because you do not like what you have been told is not a good reason for ending the relationship. It is the mentor's job to challenge your thinking and your approach, and just because you don't like her advice doesn't mean that it is automatically incorrect.

Employment Agencies

Employment agencies are designed to match you with a job. However, they are not always obliged to or interested in getting you the job that you "want" or are even suited to. If you decide to use an employment agency, it is of great importance that you align yourself with one or more agencies that will tailor their services to your needs and interests.

Be aware that you are signing up with an employment agency in a partnering relationship that is focused on getting you employment. This means that both parties are expected to put equal effort into achieving this goal. For example, the employment agency may terminate its commitment to assisting you if it believes that you are not contributing to the process.

Individuals with social-cognitive challenges such as autism spectrum disorders have increasing access to employment agencies that are specifically trained to cater to their needs and interests. A mentor or an advocate can assist in making contact with such agencies to enhance your ability to find suitable work.

■ ■ ■

XYZ Employment Agency specializes in preparing graduates and adults on the autism spectrum for the workplace and then placing them into paid employment. Jack, a man in his mid-forties with a diagnosis of autism, sought the services of the agency after years of misunderstandings at various workplaces, leading to depression. He found an employment agency staffed with people who understood his diagnosis and were very supportive in helping him to identify his strengths and assisting him in building his confidence.

Jack was assigned a caseworker, who helped him nurture his artistic abilities and direct them in a positive way. His caseworker also provided training and strategies to help Jack relate to fellow employees and suggestions for expanding his skill sets. For example, at her suggestion, Jack watched several interviews on a popular website and participated in mock interviews that he videotaped. His caseworker provided feedback on his skills in this area.

The caseworker also suggested that Jack try working as a volunteer illustrator for a local newspaper. After six months, Jack obtained a job at a graphic design company and has had his art published in many prestigious papers, journals, and websites. He is now very happy with his life due to the involvement and guidance from XYZ Employment Agency.

■ ■ ■

Hidden curriculum items related to the use of employment agencies ...

- Employment agencies and mentors each have different roles. Unless it is part of their service to do follow-up checks after securing you a job, an employment agency's service to you ends when your placement is found.

- You are expected to play a significant role in obtaining employment through an agency. The agency works as a link between you and any potential employer – in other words, they open doors to opportunity that you cannot open on your own. You have to step through that door, present well, and win the job for yourself. At the very least, employment agencies would expect their clients (you) to contribute as follows:

  1. Follow up on all opportunities that the employment agency provides, even if you think that a given job offer is "beneath you" or otherwise unsuitable. All employment adds experience to your resume.

  2. Complete any training and personal development that the employment agency recommends. This will benefit you in the long term.

  3. Attend interviews organized by the job agency with an attitude of impressing the potential employer. Attending with an attitude of "having to do it" is easily discerned by the interviewing panel. As a result, you will be seen as wasting their time and also wasting the efforts of your job agency.

  4. Actively contribute to the search for job opportunities. By becoming involved in your future, you are demonstrating to the employment agency that you are worth their efforts.

  5. Arrive on time to appointments with your caseworker. This is about respect. The job agency cannot help you if you will not help yourself.

Hidden curriculum items related to the use of employment agencies ...

- An employment agency has the right to terminate its agreement to work with you at any time. If they believe that you are not contributing sufficiently toward getting a job, they will likely decide to focus their attention on other clients who are more likely to get a job.

- Likewise, if you are not getting the service that you are expecting from an employment agency, you have every right to find another agency that will better serve your needs.

- Employment agencies are not your friends. They offer a service to you for profit. Therefore, it is unwise to invite your agent to social events, befriend them on Facebook or other social media forums, or otherwise attempt to engage with them in a social or intimate context.

- If you sign a contract with an employment agency, read it carefully. Whenever possible, avoid signing contracts that require you to pay a fee to the agency after you have obtained a job or those that stipulate that you can only work with one agency for an extended period of time.

Vocational Rehabilitation

In the United States, state vocational rehabilitation (VR) agencies provide employment-related services for individuals with disabilities, giving priority to those who have significant disabilities. Most individuals with social-cognitive challenges who have above-average intelligence quotients (IQ) are ineligible for VR services (Müller, Schuler, Burton, & Yates, 2003).

In Australia, the term vocational rehabilitation refers to measures taken to return a worker to the workforce after an injury or illness. The Australian equivalent to the U.S. VR system is the Federal Government Disability Employment Service (DES) network. Employment agencies and disability advocates tender for government grants to become DES providers with the mandate of helping people with disabilities into the workforce.

Other countries also have some form of vocational rehabilitation services that provide employment training and opportunities for people with disabilities. The exact nature of such services can be determined by asking advocates or government departments focused on disability support.

Individuals with social-cognitive challenges can seek vocational rehabilitation before they are ready or prepared to enter the workforce for the first time. Such programs will help provide the tools and confidence for the client to enter an open or supported working environment. Supported workplaces provide supervised environments where people with profound disabilities can work.

Networking

There is a common saying, "It is not what you know; it is who you know." This is often a true statement, and it applies across a wide range of scenarios.

For employment, your knowledge applicable to the job you seek is, of course, vitally important. However, it is not guaranteed to get you that job if you cannot obtain access to someone who will hire you. This is where networking comes in – the ability to connect with other people or organizations for mutual gain.

What Do We Really Mean When Talking About Networking?

So how do you network? There is no limit to your ability to get noticed by a potential employer. Family and friends are often great networking resources. Furthermore, mentors, advocates, employment agencies, social media, and vocational rehabilitation organizations are all valid networking vehicles. A conversation with a stranger can open up unforeseen connections that may not have been evident to you before. Just be mindful of the hidden curriculum for talking to strangers, such as resisting sharing personal information and being sure to conduct the conversation in a safe environment.

You can also create a network to an employer by approaching them directly – commonly referred to as "door knocking." "Door knocking" is exactly that – approaching or making an appointment at a potential employer's place of business and asking to speak to the manager or the human resources manager about potential employment opportunities within the organization. Be aware though that some companies have a policy to only accept applicants through formal means.

So how do individuals with social-cognitive challenges create networks? The answer is the same for everyone. The effort and focus involved is merely greater. However, there are networks already in place specifically designed for that purpose. The key is to identify and get involved in them.

■ ■ ■

Mary stopped by to see her sister, Jessica, to talk about her lack of success in finding a job as a veterinary assistant. Mary had earned her certification with a 4.0 grade-point average six months earlier and, despite landing several interviews, she had not been hired. Feedback from one potential employer noted that she "interviewed badly and would most likely not 'mesh well' with pet owners who visited the practice."

When Mary entered her sister's home, she was surprised to see that her sister had a guest – a neighbor from down the street. Mary was invited to join them. The three discussed several things, including Mary's lack of employment. The neighbor shared that her brother was a veterinarian and that she would be happy to arrange for Mary to meet with him.

Mary met the veterinarian the following week. Although he did not have a position for her, he offered to do a mock interview with her and introduced her to some of his veterinarian colleagues. Mary followed his interview advice and followed up on the job referrals he gave. Three months later she was employed.

■ ■ ■

Hidden curriculum items related to Mary's situation ...

- The unspoken rules for networking generally align with those for general social interactions, with the exception that the networking relationship is professional in nature. Therefore, conversations of a personal nature should be avoided.

- Keep it professional. Professional networks tend to dissolve or disappear if personal issues get involved. Your personal life should be confined to close social networks.

- If you use the door-knocking method, follow these guidelines to help ensure a successful experience:

  1. Treat it as a job interview. Dress to impress, and be confident, yet humble in your demeanor. If available, bring a small portfolio in case the employer wants to read up on you after the meeting.

  2. Avoid coming across as cocky, arrogant, or demanding. The employer is in charge. If you go with an expectation that you WILL get a job, you will likely go away very disappointed.

  3. "No" means no. If your approach is rejected, either move on or apply through conventional means. To keep coming back will be seen as "pestering," and you will be deemed unfit for employment by the organization. If you occupy the employer's reception area demanding to speak to someone about work, you will fail in your quest to get a job there, ever. Further, you will likely be escorted off the premises by security or police. In the worst case, you could get arrested, have a restraining order placed against you, or both.

  4. Door knocking is about creating opportunities. Treat it as a networking opportunity. While it may not pay off at the time, you may be remembered later on, and unexpected opportunities may be presented to you all because you made the effort to introduce yourself at some time in the past.

Hidden curriculum items related to Mary's situation ...

- Do not stalk or harass any other member in the network. If somebody cannot assist you or give you a job at the time, accept that as their position. If a member in a network feels harassed, he or she has every right to sever the link, depriving you of a future opportunity in that area.

- There is an important saying, "Don't burn your bridges." This saying applies directly to networking, especially when a professional or social relationship is ending or changing in some way. The saying is a reminder to be polite and professional at all times, even if you are being fired, reassigned, or corrected. By keeping the network link (the bridge) intact, you retain the ability to cross back over in the future if the opportunity presents itself again. In fact, your prestige in the network will be strengthened through such behavior.

- Remember that the world is a small place. *Almost any person you meet could either be (a) a potential mentor or (b) have a connection that might help you find a job.* The person who accidentally bumps into you, making you spill your coffee at a coffee shop, could be the supervisor of the personnel department of a company you would like to work for. So, remember to always project the image you would like potential employers to see. *Keep this in mind when interacting with others.*

- Networking is about opportunities. The more networks you have, the more opportunities you get, and the more successful you are likely to be.

Social Media

Social networking can be a great asset for finding a job. It can also undo all of your efforts. The difference is in how you navigate the hidden curriculum of the social network.

All social networking vehicles, of which there are hundreds, depending on your interest, are in the public domain. Even if you are very diligent about whom your "friends" are, anything you post on those sites can become accessible to anyone, anywhere.

These forums have become a very powerful tool for employers to use when vetting potential employees. An innocent "friend" request can lead to an inspection of your posted content and opinions. Very quickly the employer can ascertain who you "really" are as opposed to who you purport to be in the job application or interview. For example, presenting as a respectable, professional applicant at an interview while showing off on Facebook as an inconsiderate party animal with deviant tendencies will likely lead an interviewer with knowledge of the Facebook profile to disregard the credibility of the applicant.

The best known social media platforms are Facebook, Twitter, and LinkedIn.

Facebook is designed for social networking. Consequently, Facebook users tend to make posts and share links of a personal nature about activities, interests, and opinions. However, many businesses use Facebook to attract and engage customers (Bakshy, Marlow, Rosenn, & Adamic, n.d.).

Twitter is a social networking platform designed to communicate thoughts, feelings, and activities using a maximum of 140 characters. It can be viewed as communicating your "thought at the moment." It is primarily associated with celebrities who communicate with their fans as a group. A study of the content of tweets (Twitter communication) revealed that 40% was "pointless babble" and 38% was "conversational." Only 8% of tweets had "pass-along value" (Kelly, 2009). It is also a very easy way for one to metaphorically "put one's foot in one's mouth." Many people have found themselves in serious trouble due to a poorly thought-out tweet.

LinkedIn is designed specifically for professional networking. Advertised as the world's largest network of its type, LinkedIn uses a "gate-access approach," whereby contact with a professional requires a preexisting direct relationship or a mutual relationship with a third party. LinkedIn can then be used to find jobs and follow specific companies to determine whether they are searching for candidates.

Other professional networking sites include:

(a) Networking for Professionals (www.networkingforprofes-sionals.com) – offers online networking and business events

(b) Ryze (www.ryze.com) – links business professionals, in particular, new entrepreneurs

(c) Xing (www.xing.com) – enables small-world networking for professionals.

The hidden curriculum of social media is vast, and different rules apply to different vehicles within the social network. For example, professional networking rules differ from those of online social or special interest forums.

■ ■ ■

Edwardo held a position at an accounting firm. He worked hard and produced excellent results. Edwardo was fascinated with Facebook and often posted random thoughts on his wall, sometimes about work-related issues. Among his online friends were some of his fellow employees. Most of Edwardo's comments were innocuous, even funny. However, on one occasion he felt that he had been victimized by his line manager. The incident in question was minor to most observers. His manager had reprimanded him for making an administrative mistake on a client's tax return. The mistake would not have gotten the client into trouble with the IRS.

Edwardo posted his feelings on Facebook along with the client's name and his opinions about his line manager. Some of his opinions were spiteful and demeaning. These posts were brought to the attention of Edwardo's line manager who, upset by the "attack" on his character and the use of a client's name, passed the information on to the managing director of the human resources department. Edwardo was summarily dismissed for breaching corporate policy.

■ ■ ■

Hidden curriculum items related to social media ...

- Keep any personal opinions to yourself regarding other people's race, creed, culture, minority status, etc. Do not post them on social networking sites. Whether fairly or unfairly, you will be judged according to the opinions you present.

- Recognize that you risk claims of slander if you vilify another person on your social media page and could become the defendant of a lawsuit and, therefore, exposed to major damages.

- Be aware of what your "friends" are posting onto your wall or onto your profile page. Delete or hide a post immediately if the posting does not fit with the image you want to project to the world.

- Keep in mind that you are responsible for your social media profile. You have the right to add or delete any content or "friends" at any time. You are also responsible for the conduct of your "friends" on your profile page.

- Avoid cursing or antisocial behavior on your profile page even if you implicitly trust every one of your "friends" to protect your privacy.

- Be aware that your future or current employer, or someone that they know, could also be a "friend" on your social media page. Your conduct is always on display, even after you have left your place of work, so be very careful about the photographs and content you post. Some companies view a potential employee's social networking site before deciding whether to offer him or her a job.

- Do not join groups or subscribe to pages that contain content that might be considered controversial by employers or colleagues.

- Unless your job description includes browsing social networking pages, limit your use of social media to your personal time. Such browsing without permission while at work is, in some places, a dismissible offense.

Using Your Natural Resources

To make use of your natural resources, you must first know what they are and how you can access them. "Natural resources," by definition, refers to the mineral wealth of a nation. When the term is applied to an individual, it refers to his or her inherent knowledge, interests, and abilities as well as any external sources that are available for support. Therefore, mentors, employment agencies, networking contacts, friends, and family can all be used as external natural resources.

As securing and maintaining a job is ultimately up to the individual, it is his or her internal natural resources that are of greatest importance. Often a topic of special interest or a favorite hobby can open up great and enjoyable employment opportunities.

The following is a list of special interests and possible job matches. The list is provided as an example only, and is far from exhaustive. What is your special interest? What careers do you think will match or even complement that special interest?

Table 2.1
Special Interests and Potential Job Matches

Special Interest	Possible Job Match
Dinosaurs	Paleontologist Paleontologist assistant
History	Historical librarian Genealogical society researcher Historical researcher
Archaeology	Archaeologist Archaeologist assistant Museum employee
Drawing and/or Artist	Graphic designer Illustrator Architect
Planes	Pilot Navigator Air traffic controller Aeronautical engineer

Table 2.1 (cont.)

Special Interest	Possible Job Match
Insects	Entomologist Gardener
Autism Spectrum	Advocate Mentor Educator
Bridges	Construction laborer Crane driver
Cars	Mechanic Mechanical engineer Traffic counter Car museum attendant Car wash attendant

Explore your options. You will be surprised by what you may uncover. Then explore how you can secure a career that complements your special interest. Use your mentors to help identify how your interest can be converted into an employment opportunity.

■ ■ ■

From an early age, Dallas had developed an intense special interest in trains. As such, it became a daily ritual for his parents to take Dallas to the train station so that he could watch the trains. Here he would diligently record the number and type of carriages, the make and model of the engines, and the times of arrival and departure so that he could compare them to the official schedule when he got home.

Dallas's parents recognized their son's special interest as a natural resource and continued to be supportive and proactive in its development. For example, they bought books, models, and videos of trains that served to increase Dallas's knowledge.

With encouragement from his parents, Dallas chose mechanical engineering as his major in college so he could help design and build better trains. His parents also helped him identify companies that employed mechanical engineers who specialized in locomotives and approached most of them with the goal of securing an internship for their son.

*After a successful internship experience, Dallas secured
a job with ABC Engineering when he graduated, and is now
well respected by his peers and supervisors alike for his
knowledge of train mechanics.*

■ ■ ■

Most hidden curriculum items for the use of natural resources
are covered in other sections, such as the Role of Mentors and
Networking. However, some are unique to this topic, including the
following:

Hidden curriculum items related to natural resources ...

- Enhance your natural resources to become even better at what you do. This, in turn, will increase your value to potential employers.
- Continue to explore your natural resources through research, attending meetings or conferences, and talking with others who have the same interests.
- Find out what careers meet your interests and then pursue training and networking opportunities to link up with organizations that offer those careers.

Creating a Resume

Once you have identified potential jobs, it is time to apply for
them. Use your mentors, employment agencies (if applicable), and
your network contacts to assist you in preparing a resume and a
cover letter that will give you the best chance of being noticed by a
prospective employer.

Your resume should reflect your education, job experience (including volunteer positions and internships), and specialized training. When appropriate, for example, in socially oriented employment
fields, you may want to include some personal information about
yourself. Websites that provide good examples of resumes include

29

http://www.bestsampleresume.com/, and http://www.freeresumesa-mples.org/. There are also many free resume templates available on-line, including http://www.resumetemplates.org/ and http://jobsearch.about.com/cs/resumesamples/a/resumetemplate.htm.

Cover Letter

When you mail or submit a resume, be sure to include a cover letter. Whenever possible, tailor the letter to the specific job. A template for a tailor-made cover letter may be found at http://job-search.about.com/od/morejobletters/a/jobappletter.htm.

The first paragraph of the letter states the purpose for the letter, including where you heard or read about the position, and names the position you are interested in obtaining. The second paragraph shows your interest in the job with at least three specific state-ments of how your qualifications match the job requirements – use terminology that appears in the advertisement. The final paragraph contains a reference to your resume and your contact informa-tion. Templates may be found at http://jobsearch.about.com/od/coverlettersamples/a/coverlettsample.htm, as well as at http://www.resume-resource.com/cover-template.html.

Most applications must now be submitted online. However, this does not affect the above information. It is good practice to append your resume with a cover letter to the online application if it is pos-sible to do so.

Application Forms

The application form is an important component of the job ap-plication process as it provides specific information to the employ-er about the applicant. A submission for employment will likely not be considered if the application form is left out, regardless of how impressive your resume or cover letter is.

Be honest with your answers but also be mindful that some of the information you enter onto the application form may lead the employer to discriminate against you. Some personal information that may be asked for on the form is optional. Leave any detailed information for the interview.

There are many hidden curriculum items related to the application process. Some have been covered in previous sections. In addition ...

Hidden curriculum items related to creating a resume ...

- Develop a standard resume. Then tailor your application and cover letter to each individual job. This may include highlighting aspects of your employment history for some jobs and downplaying them for others, depending on the position you are applying for.

- Ask several people if they can serve as references for you. Typical references include bosses or supervisors (for both paid and volunteer positions), former professors/instructors, and mentors. Select the three most applicable to the position. Typically, resumes include the statement, "References will be provided upon request." This means that you will be ready to submit the references when requested by the interviewer.

- Keep your cover letter brief but long enough to cover the main points. Interviewers are busy people and will likely discard an application that will take a long time to read. Likewise, a cover letter that is lacking detail may convey laziness or disinterest on behalf of the applicant and, therefore, may also be discarded.

- Ensure that all of the major requirements stipulated in the position description are covered in some form in either your cover letter or resume. Again, be brief and to the point.

- Even the best applicant sometimes fails to get the job. The selection of who is employed is entirely at the employer's discretion. If you are not chosen, let that opportunity go and focus on other opportunities.

- Apply concurrently for as many jobs as possible. It is far better to be in a position of having to decline an offer if you have already secured another job than having no other options in play should your application be unsuccessful.

- Always be polite, respectful, and professional in your application. An employer is likely to ignore an applicant who appears disrespectful or unprofessional.

Summary

Enhance your job preparedness and prospects through mentors, advocates, and employment agencies that will support you in your career goals and aspirations. Use everything at your disposal to create a strong resume and a large supportive network to maximize your chances of success.

Consider your interests when job hunting. A job matched with your interests could be rewarding and enjoyable for you and for your employer.

Chapter Three

Having an Interview

Often the final hurdle to overcome in the application process is securing an interview and, in that interview, convincing the employer that you are the candidate that they need. Getting the interview is the culmination of the steps in the previous chapter. That is, you first understand yourself and your natural resources to identify a desirable career path, often using mentors and networking for guidance and vocational rehabilitation for assistance. Then, you identify what jobs are available using mentors, social media, employment agencies, and networking.

The job interview is the most complex step in the job-searching process with hidden rules and expectations that can change depending on the job position, the corporate culture of the company, and the personal beliefs of the individuals on the interviewing panel.

When advertising for a person to fill a vacancy, an employer already has a concept of the ideal employee for the role, which includes criteria regarding personality, skills, and experience. The interview is one of the employer's most effective tools for matching applicants to those criteria.

Other aspects of the employer's concept are more subtle, either intentionally or otherwise. For example, an employer may be looking for an employee who fits a particular personality profile or who has experience in certain aspects that are not stated in the job description. One way in which an interviewee can stand out among the other applicants is to identify and address some of the hidden criteria in addition to the stated requirements, thereby increasing his or her chance of success by matching more fully the employer's concept. Researching the company's culture and talking to some of its employees are ways of identifying some of the hidden expectations.

The interview process also serves another role. Companies are often searching for employees who will give them a commercial edge over their competitors. Therefore, they attempt to identify individuals with unique skills and abilities that are complementary to the company's goals and direction. The most effective way for an employer to identify such an individual is through the job interview process.

What are the hidden curriculum rules for the job interview and how can these rules be identified? A simple Internet search such as "what not to do at a job interview" will reveal the source material for many hidden curriculum rules. Also, mentors, employment agencies, advocates, and trainers specialize in preparing job applicants for the job interview. Any of these resources can be found through job placement guides, Internet searches, or recommendation from someone you know.

In the following, the hidden curriculum for the job interview is divided into sections addressing presentation, manner, responses, and follow-up, as well as a special section on the hidden curriculum for the interviewer.

Hidden curriculum items related to presentation for the job interview (what to wear) ...

- Identify the dress code of the company. If you present yourself in a style similar, not identical, to those in the business, you may be seen as conforming to the company's vision. This can be done by viewing staff photos on the company's website or in its brochures.

- Dress for the part. Suits, for both men and women, are highly recommended for corporate, administration, or retail positions – commonly referred to as white-collar professions. Aim for a business casual look for industrial or labor jobs – this may include dress jeans (not torn or faded) and a collared shirt for men and women, although women may choose to wear a dress or a skirt in lieu of jeans. If in doubt, ask your mentor or the company's human resources department what their expectations are for interview dress code.

- Do not under-dress, as this can be construed as disinterest or lack of respect for the interviewing panel.

- Piercings and body art should be removed or covered for the interview unless they are applicable to the job, such as tattoo artist, beautician, or a position at a trendy bar. Otherwise, unless they are discreet in nature, piercings and body art may be viewed as "unprofessional" and sometimes as disrespectful of authority.

- Be sure your personal hygiene is impeccable. Body odor, bad breath, messy hair, an unshaven face (for men), unclean teeth, etc., are often viewed as offensive or disrespectful by the interviewing panel.

Hidden curriculum items related to mannerisms for the job interview (how to behave) ...

- Arrive at least 10 minutes early for the interview and never interrupt the interview except for an emergency.

- To comply with the previous rule, ensure that the following is taken care of before entering the interview:
  - Turn off your mobile phone and any other electronic device that could be distracting.
  - Use the restroom at least 15 minutes before the interview.
  - If you are chewing gum, tobacco, or anything else, remove it from your mouth and dispose of it in a suitable place. The same rule applies to anything that you are sucking or chewing on.
  - Take any vital prescription medication or other treatment.

- Keep in mind that the interview begins the moment you enter the building and ends the moment you leave it. Companies often use the receptionist as a secret interviewer. As a result, your manner and behavior in a "public" area away from the interview room can and often does get reported to the interviewer and is used in assessing your "true" persona.

- Go to the interview even if you are feeling a bit ill. This shows dedication. If the interviewer is uncomfortable about interviewing you in such a state, it is up to him to reschedule – at least you showed up.

> **Exception to the Above Rule**
>
> If you are contagious or otherwise bed-ridden, send your apologies and a letter from your doctor addressed to the interviewer and explaining why you cannot attend and requesting a rescheduled meeting. This demonstrates integrity and respect and will be valued highly by most companies.

- Be aware of your body language. The way in which you present during an interview can and often does have an effect on the interviewer. For example, crossing your arms may be construed as defensiveness or as an obstructive gesture. Wandering eyes may be seen as a sign of boredom or distraction. Role play interview scenarios with a mentor or with a trainer who is skilled in body language techniques to learn how to best present yourself in an interview situation.

Hidden curriculum items related to responses for the job interview (what to say and how to say it) ...

- BE YOURSELF. The interviewer is looking to hire a real person, not a fictional representation of who you think they want. You might get the job through deceptive means, but you will not keep it for long once the deception is uncovered.

- Do not assume that the job is yours just because you have landed an interview, as this can be taken as arrogance and works against your chances of success. Be confident and polite. Use phrases such as "If I am hired for this position ..."

- Avoid slang terms, profanities, or stereotypical language, such as calling the interviewer "girlfriend" or referring to your previous employer as "an ass." This may be taken as impolite and disrespectful. Speak clearly and concisely in the language of the interviewer.

- When asked to talk about yourself, keep the dialogue brief and on topics associated with your professional growth applicable to the position that you are being interviewed for. Such topics include certifications, training, experiences, etc. Be prepared to very briefly discuss your personal interests if asked. A succinct statement such as "I enjoy collecting stamps and reading – primarily history" is appropriate. Any volunteer activities, such as helping out at a food bank or playing piano at an assisted living facility, are also appropriate personal interests to mention. Unless applying for a job that creates or sells gaming devices, it would probably not be beneficial to indicate that your personal interest includes playing online or video games. Avoid personal topics that could lead the company to discriminate against you – refer to the last part of this section for more details.

- Use positive language and expressions when asked about former employers. If you show that you hold negative feelings about a past employer, the interviewer may think that you could, in the future, show the same feelings about the company for which you are being interviewed. For example, referring to a past employer in a positive way could be "I value my experience with XYZ; they taught me a great deal about teamwork." A negative approach might be "XYZ were useless. They never respected my contribution and I'm glad to be rid of them."

Hidden curriculum items related to responses for the job interview (what to say and how to say it) ...

- Avoid asking what the company can offer you in terms of salary or benefits. This can be seen as rude and obnoxious. The employer is giving you an opportunity to be hired – demonstrate gratitude for that opportunity. In almost all circumstances, the employer will bring up issues of salary and benefits before you accept or refuse the position.

- Know your strengths and your areas in need of improvement. This will help when asked, "What are your strengths and weaknesses?" Prepare yourself for this question. "What can you do better and how?" "What do you do well and how can you get even better at it?" Knowing the answer to both of these questions in advance shows that you have considered aspects of yourself concerning continual growth and improvement.

  Reminder: Avoid dwelling on your weaknesses. The interviewer wants you to "sell" yourself, not to dissuade her from hiring you!

- Avoid showing ignorance about what the company produces. Your research prior to the interview should have informed you of this. Therefore, do not ask the interviewer questions about the company that you could easily learn by yourself by looking at their website or brochures.

- Prepare for how to answer the question, "Do you have any questions?" Do your research about the company ahead of time and prepare at least three questions about the future direction and aspirations of the company. This will demonstrate that you have knowledge about the company and that you are interested in taking an active part in their progress. Visit websites to prepare for this question. Just type "do you have any questions at a job interview" in your Internet search engine for some inspiration.

The following three websites provide excellent resources for practicing and honing your answers to common interview questions.

http://www.jobsite.co.uk/bemyinterviewer/. This website has recorded the interview questions of experienced professionals across a broad range of organizations in the United Kingdom. The interviewers also explain what they are looking for in an answer to those questions. This is a strong website for learning interview skills and is highly recommended.

http://www.kent.ac.uk/careers/interviews/mockivs. htm. This site gives a range of questions and suggested answers across a large array of career paths. You can choose to read a suggested answer before typing in your own response.

http://myinterviewsimulator.com/. This is a good simulator that gives audible questions and written suggestions on how to prepare for and respond to those questions. Many basic and more specific interview questions are provided. You can also test your skills in the interview simulator.

Hidden curriculum items related to the dreaded meltdown (how to avoid it while in an interview) ...

- Find out what keeps you calm while allowing you to focus on the interviewer. Headphones, sunglasses, chewing gum, etc., are not recommended therapies to employ during an interview. Small stress balls or other sensory devices that can be concealed within your hand are acceptable, as long as they do not distract the interview process. Find something subtle and effective.

- Find a mentor, coach, or friend who can train you in achieving a positive state that enhances your calmness during an interview. Practice the technique in situations that you find stressful to prove to yourself that it works. Then, if you feel your calm fading during the job interview, re-access the state for achieving positivity and calm and continue with the interview.

- Relax. The interviewer is there to help you through the process. You are at the interview because you are deemed capable of doing the job. Trust in your ability to demonstrate that capability.

Hidden curriculum items related to interviewing via Skype or webcam ...

- Remember that the presentation rules still apply – dress and groom yourself appropriately.

- Remove any visual distractions from the background or put up a blank screen behind you. Otherwise, the interviewer can use anything that is in the visual field of the webcam to include in his assessment of you.

- Be aware of your mannerisms. Being in the comfort of your own home may cause you to be more relaxed, such that unconscious behaviors like nose picking, eye rubbing, scratching, etc., become more prevalent. Behave as if you were in the same room as the interviewer – because you are, through a webcam.

- Turn off or mute any devices such as radios, cell phones, televisions, etc., that could create distracting background noise.

- If you have a roommate, partner, or family sharing living space with you, inform them of your interview and ask that they not disturb you during this time. If possible, ask them to leave during this time so that their activities do not disturb the process.

- Do not play computer games, read emails, type letters, or work on anything else on your computer or otherwise during the interview. The interviewer wants your complete attention. To be distracted is a sign of disrespect and disinterest.

- Remember that the interview concludes when the webcam connection is closed. Be very sure that this is the case before making off-the-cuff remarks about the interviewer, the company, etc. If the line is still open and you voice such comments, you could ruin any chance you had of getting the job.

- Apply all other hidden curriculum rules for the job interview.

Hidden curriculum items related to job interview follow-up (what to do when the job interview is over) ...

The following also applies to applications that have failed to get to the interview stage.

- At the end of the interview, ask what the follow-up process will be. That is, when and how can you expect to hear back from the interviewer? If you have not heard back within the timeframe given, wait another day or two and then make a polite inquiry to the appropriate person. If you harass the company for an answer, they will likely label you as a pest and remove you from consideration.

- Immediately after the interview, write and mail a brief note thanking the interviewer for the interview. Sample thank you letters may be found at http://jobsearch.about.com/od/thankyouletters/a/samplethankyou.htm.

- If you receive a notice that you were not hired for the position, move on to the next prospect. It is okay to respectfully ask for feedback at this stage. It is not okay to demand it.

- You have a right to ask for feedback from an employer for whom your application has failed to secure an interview. However, the employer may ignore or decline your request. If they decline, thank them and move on. If they do not respond, move on. To do otherwise could be seen as harassment, and this could impact future employment opportunities. The following should be considered when requesting feedback:
  - Find out when interviews are expected to be held. If you have not received a request for an interview within a week following the advised timeframe, then first check that the interviews have not been delayed and then, if it is obvious that you have been overlooked, request feedback at that time.
  - The best format for a feedback request is letter or e-mail. Keep the request professional and to the point, stating the position applied for and politely asking for feedback on your application with the stated intention of learning from the process.
  - Feedback can also be sought over the phone. Be mindful that some employers find this too confronting.

- If you receive an acceptance – congratulations! The terms of the acceptance will usually instruct you on what to do next.

Know Your Rights

Most Western nations have in place anti-discrimination legislation. These laws apply to most situations in society, including the job interview.

It is, therefore, illegal for an interviewer to ask you any question that could lead you to be discriminated against. The list of illegal question topics is long and includes such items as maiden and middle names, marital status, age, health, gender, sexual orientation, race, cultural background, religious beliefs, place of birth, etc. Basically, anything of a personal nature is off limits. For further information, visit http://pattyinglishms.hubpages.com/hub/Illegal_Questions.

There are exceptions to these laws, some of which are covered in the hidden curriculum items below. One exception is certain government agencies where national security is a high priority. Another is a company that cannot employ minors – asking if you are over 18 is permitted in this circumstance. However, they still cannot ask for your actual age.

- Interviewers cannot ask you about sexual harassment or how you would deal with it if confronted by a situation involving sexual harassment. If it happens, politely redirect the interview to the topic of the job on offer and what you have to offer the company. If the interviewer presses the question, again politely advise him or her that you are not going to answer the question as it has no relevance to the position on offer.

- Avoid using the word "illegal" if confronted by discriminating questions. This will create a state of conflict in the interview and will seriously limit your chances of employment. Instead, be polite yet firm saying something like, "I prefer to keep my professional and personal lives separate" or "why do you ask?"

- **Warning** – if you volunteer information freely that fits into any discriminatory category, then that category is now open for the interviewer to explore further. Think carefully before you disclose anything personal about yourself.

- If you are not hired because the employer has discriminated against you based on information given, then you may have legal recourse. Always seek legal advice before bringing up accusations of this type, because such recourse could give you a reputation as litigious, making it more difficult to secure work. Often, it is better to walk away, knowing that you have narrowly avoided working for a company that might discriminate against you.

Summary

The job interview is the most complex step in the job-search process with hidden rules and expectations that can change depending on the job position, the corporate culture of the company, and the personal beliefs of the individuals on the interviewing panel.

Companies are often searching for employees who will give them a commercial edge over their competitors. Therefore, they attempt to identify individuals with unique skills and abilities that are complementary to the company's goals and direction. The most effective way for an employer to identify such an individual is through the job interview process.

Chapter Four

The Hidden Curriculum Beyond the Job Match

The job match is considered crucial for successful employment of anybody, but especially so for adults with social-cognitive challenges, including those with autism spectrum disorders (ASD), who tend to thrive in jobs whose requirements match their personal strengths and preferences (Schutte, 2009).

Grandin and Duffy (2008) identified jobs that are compatible with the learning style of visual thinkers and nonvisual thinkers. They have also identified vocations that are less suitable (see Table 4.1).

Table 4.1
Job Matches for Visual and Nonvisual Thinkers Who Have a High Need for Structure and Predictability

Good Job Matches		Poor Job Matches
Visual Thinkers	**Nonvisual Thinkers**	
Draft technician	Accountant	Cashier
Photographer	Librarian	Short-order cook
Animal trainer	Computer programmer	Waiter
Graphic artist	Engineer	Casino employee
Jewelry maker	Journalist	Taxi dispatcher
Web designer	Inventory controller	Air traffic controller
Veterinary technician	Statistician	Futures trader
Auto mechanic	Bank teller	Receptionist
Machine-maintenance worker	Copy editor	Airline ticket agent
Lighting technician	Laboratory technician	Administrative assistant
Landscape designer		

Researchers Howlin, Alcock, and Burkin (2005) attempted to quantify the concept of job matching for adults with high-functioning autism spectrum disorders (HFASD) by identifying the types of work held by 89 adults with HFASD. Table 4.2 highlights the type of work, examples of jobs within each type, and the percentage of adults who held this type of position.

Table 4.2
Employment of 89 High-Ability Adults With Autism

Type of Work	Examples of Jobs	% of Jobs
Administration/technical	Statistician, chemist, research officer, photographer	8.0%
Administrative assistance	Archivist, accounting, etc.	22.0%
Technical assistance	Librarian, financial, technical officer	13.0%
Data entry	Keyboard operator, data input clerk	6.0%
Data management	IT analyst, web designer	3.5%
Office work	Clerical assistant in offices, banks, etc.	19%
Secretarial	Administrative assistant in hospitals, universities	1.5%
Shop work	Customer service representative, travel agent, public transportation driver, cashier	8.0%
Stockroom	Shelf stocker	6.0%
Postal work	Mail deliverer/sorting clerk	4.0%
"Other"	Support worker, preschool aide, messenger, gardener	7.0%
Catering	Chef, kitchen hand	1.5%
Cleaning	Custodian, bus person in restaurant, housekeeper	0.5%

Many of these jobs have structure, routine, and focus on a special interest, all crucial attributes when finding suitable employment for individuals with ASD (Hagner & Cooney, 2005). Researchers and practitioners further assert that adults with HFA are successful in jobs that require few or very structured social interactions. For example, jobs that incorporate mentors (see Chapter Two) who clearly specify job responsibilities, expectations, assumptions, and rules provide the predictability necessary for employees on the spectrum. Table 4.3 lists a series of factors that create employment success (Dew & Alan, 2007; Hagner & Cooney, 2005; Hurlbutt & Chalmers, 2004).

Table 4.3
Factors That Lead to Successful Employment for Adults on the Spectrum

- Consistent schedule and job responsibilities
- Ongoing relationship with a mentor, who explains specific job duties, responsibilities, expectations, and rules related to productivity, breaks, tasks, social interactions, and how to ask for help
- Predictable social demands
- System to keep track of work progress
- Predictable routines for lunch, breaks, and other unstructured times during the workday
- Time before the beginning of the workday to organize self and tasks
- Direct communication with opportunities for clarification and verification
- Reminders and reassurances
- Coworkers who initiate interactions and help "keep an eye out" for the employee
- If support providers are involved, a method to transfer these services and supports to the mentor and fellow employees

Adults with classic autism and with HFASD rank the lowest among all disability groups in employment, with 6% and 12%, respectively, having jobs (http://www.autism.org.uk/living-with-autism/employment.aspx). This, combined with the short job tenure of high-functioning adults on the autism spectrum, makes it clear that the concept of job matching must be broadened to take into consideration the *hidden curriculum beyond the job match*. That is, the traditional notion of job matching is only one component since many adults can easily master the job task itself. Among those who get hired, many find that the work environment, along with all the complex everyday situations generated by the various players, tips the scales in such a way as to become the deal breaker in terms of keeping the job.

In this chapter, we will look at elements of the work-related hidden curriculum that are known to pose challenges for individuals with autism and other social-cognitive difficulties who otherwise meet the specific "technical" requirements of a given job. These include (a) arriving at work ready to engage, (b) managing stress to maintain engagement throughout the workday, and (c) interpreting and reacting to social demands.

Arriving at Work Ready to Engage

A hidden curriculum rule seldom expressed until broken is that employees are expected to arrive at the workplace on time and ready to engage in the workday. For most employees, this means that it is best to arrive well rested, personal hygiene accounted for, dressed comfortably and in accordance with the dress code, and ready to turn their attention to the workplace while putting personal concerns and matters on hold during work hours.

Individuals with ASD must often bring intentionality to arriving at work ready to engage because their neurology does not automatically regulate their systems (physical, sensory, emotional, movement) efficiently (Endow, 2012). For example, more than 70% of those with ASD experience sleep disturbances (Polimeni, Richdale, & Francis, 2005; Rzepecka, McKenzie, McClure, & Murphy, 2011).

Most people experience an occasional bad night's sleep and go to work tired, but they are usually able to manage getting through the day, knowing they will catch up on their sleep by taking a nap when they get home or by going to bed early that night. But for many with ASD, sleep irregularities extend far beyond the occasional sleepless night, impacting their ability to be at their best during the workday. When this is the case, it is important to determine how to get a good night's rest. Helpful strategies include establishing a consistent bedtime routine, avoiding caffeine in the late afternoon/evening, taking a relaxing bath, listening to soothing music, and consulting your physician about using an over-the-counter sleep medication.

Another area that often requires thoughtful consideration is the routine before leaving home for work. Most people find it helpful to have a before-work routine that includes hygiene/bathing, dressing, and eating a meal. Many find it helpful to add in other activities, such as cleaning up and organizing the house, checking email, watching the news, taking a walk, or engaging in some other physical activity. Often, individuals with ASD do not naturally engage in these typical everyday routines but instead must bring intentional thought to establishing them. It is important to allow enough time before leaving home to go through a daily routine that allows you to be ready to work once you arrive at your place of employment. Once it is intentionally established, this sort of routine helps to meet regulation needs.

It is often necessary to engage in similar routines after work. Many with ASD find that they are unable to schedule social events during the week because, added to the demands of the workday, it is a recipe for overload and dysregulation. Others are able to add limited social events or an event that involves only a few people or occurs in a quiet atmosphere. It is important to identify how much social activity to include during the workweek without compromising the ability to be efficient and effective at work.

Another consideration to take into account is how many outside-of-the-home errands you can add into the workweek and still maintain the regulation needed for successful employment. Many individuals with ASD choose to do errands on their days off so as not to have to add them into the workday.

In addition to errands, household tasks need to be taken into consideration. When considerable time has to be spent on regulatory activities on a daily basis, it is often desirable to do house cleaning, laundry, grocery shopping, and cooking on days off.

■　■　■

Tellis sets his alarm to go off two hours before he has to leave the house on workdays. He wakes at 5 a.m., has his coffee while checking his email, and plays an online jigsaw puzzle game until 5:45. He then prepares breakfast, which consists of a bowl of instant oatmeal, a banana, and some yogurt. He eats his breakfast in the living room while watching the morning news on TV. When the weather report is over, Tellis puts his dishes in the dishwasher, rinses out the coffee pot, brush-

es his teeth, shaves, applies deodorant, and dresses. (He showers in the evening.) Then he straightens his bedroom, combs his hair, and puts on his watch. Tellis checks the time. He is almost always ready by 6:45, which allows him to take the longest route to work.

Tellis works in the mailroom of a large corporation in a high-rise building. He enjoys walking to work because it provides him with an opportunity for regulation. He has three different routes to choose from, each taking a slightly differ-ent amount of time. When it is raining or too cold to walk, he drives his car to work and takes his walk in the halls on the 19th floor, where most workers have not yet arrived.

He arrives at his workstation 10-15 minutes before he actually has to start working. He chooses to do this because he likes to get a heads-up on the work task posting for the day – a sheet of paper hung in the work area that tells the task line-up for the day. Most of the day follows a routine, but for one hour mid-morning he has to do one of three dif-ferent tasks.

Tellis likes to see the day's task posting, hang up his jacket, and go to the break room to watch the very end of the sports segment of the morning news. He then goes to his workstation, greeting two coworkers along the way. When his workday is over, he walks home.

Tellis also has a routine for his weekday evenings. When arriving home after work, he spends some time playing com-puter games while drinking a coke. He then fixes his meal and eats it while watching the evening news. On Tuesdays and Thursdays, he goes swimming at the YMCA after dinner. On Mondays and Wednesdays, he generally watches TV for an hour or two, after which he enjoys being on Facebook, calling his sister, mother, or friends on the phone, playing computer games, or using apps on his iPad. On Friday evenings, Tellis and two buddies meet up at the mall to eat in the food court. Sometimes they go to a movie at the theater in the mall, at other times they play games in the Game Hangout or look in some of the stores. Even though he enjoys this weekly outing, he knows that it would not be a wise thing to do on a week-night when he has to work the next day. He is awake for a few extra hours on Friday nights because the mall environment tends to rev up his system. He needs to be home a few hours in his quiet condo before he can go to bed and fall asleep. Tellis has learned what he needs to do to keep himself well regulated during the week so he can arrive at work ready to do a good job.

■ ■ ■

Hidden curriculum items related to Tellis' situation ...

- Employees must arrive at work ready to work.
- Employees must arrive early enough to get settled in (hang up jacket, say hello to coworkers, use the bathroom, etc.) so that they are ready to begin working at the starting time.
- Before accepting invitations or engaging in activities, employees must factor in how social activities during off-work hours will affect their performance during the workweek.

Managing Stress to Maintain Engagement Throughout the Workday

Because their neurology often does not automatically notice stress signals and keep their body regulated, most individuals with ASD have to bring intentionality to maintaining engagement and managing stress throughout their workday. To do so, they need a way to monitor their stress levels because they often do not know when they are becoming dysregulated. In addition, it is helpful, as a proactive measure, to have a predetermined regulation plan to implement for each level of stress. This helps to manage the impact of the ASD in the context of the ever-changing demands encountered during the workday.

■　■　■

Even though Lilia enjoys her job as a tax accountant, she is continually challenged by stress. In order to understand her stress, Lilia has learned to identify stress by her behavior. As her stress level increases, her visual sense becomes overwhelmed. While Lilia initially could not track this in real time, once she identified the behaviors she engaged in, she had no difficulty knowing which level of stress she was experiencing at any given time and was able to take precautions accordingly.

When her stress level is low, Lilia takes off her glasses. She knows her stress level is medium when she rubs her eyes, and when she needs to use tissues to wipe her watering eyes her stress level is high.

Using concrete, easily observable behavior indicators matched to stress levels enables Lilia to track her stress level accurately, which in turn allows her to employ regulation strategies known to be most effective at each level of stress. Table 4.4 illustrates this in the first column of Lilia's self-regulation plan.

Lilia uses this plan periodically throughout the day, employing the self-regulation techniques she knows will be most helpful to her according to her stress level at the time. Besides using her stress level to manage her regulation needs, Lilia has matched each of her stress levels with a personal reminder of how she will react to various situations. For example, like most with ASD, as Lilia's stress level increases, she becomes less flexible at dealing with perceived change or interruption in her routine/plan. Lilia finds that it is easier to outsmart this aspect of her ASD by being ready to implement a personal reminder (see column three in Table 4.4) according to her stress level.

Table 4.4
Lilia's Self-Regulation Plan

Stress Level	Regulation Plan	Personal Reminder
High: Clenching teeth, eyes watering, cannot understand meaning of written words	Take formal break time: • Close and lock office door • Turn off ringer and lights • Lie on yoga mat with iPod • Listen to 13-minute nature music selections	The unexpected will hit me like a big lightening bolt. Do: Pause, take a deep breath. Inhibit blurting, "No!" Say: "Let me think about this and get back with you."
Medium: Extraneous drumming on computer keyboard, rubbing eyes, lag time between reading and understanding written words	Increase regulation assistance: • Turn on white noise maker • Switch to lamp lighting as opposed to overhead fluorescent light • Take a short walk (i.e., use restroom, deposit outgoing mail, refresh drink)	The unexpected will annoy me. Do: Intentionally smile; exhibit positive, friendly body language. Inhibit annoyance. Say: "Okay," "Yes," "I'll add that to my list," or "I'll get back with you in just a moment. Do you mind if I ask any questions I may have then?"
Low: Rubs fabric of clothing between fingers, takes off glasses, momentary lag time between hearing and understanding spoken words	Employ a regulation aid: • Close office door • Chew gum • Drink coffee or other beverage	I am able to handle the unexpected Do: Set the visual timer on my iPhone at 30 min to do next stress-level check. Engage in normal conversation style. Say: When in doubt, remember to comment to show that you are listening by saying, "thanks," "interesting," "sorry," "I see," "okay," or some other generic comment.
None	Enjoy my stress-free status!	Continue to follow my CAPS (see p. 55)

■ ■ ■

For those who need even more support, it often helps to develop a road map that shows precisely which supports they need in each challenging situation across the workday for optimal functioning. This will allow the employee to be as productive as possible in work tasks while managing the hidden curriculum of the work environment, a combination that is often the deal-maker in keeping a job.

This road map, known as the Comprehensive Autism Planning System (CAPS; Henry & Myles, 2007), is driven by the principles of self-determination. CAPS not only addresses self-regulation and the hidden curriculum, it also takes into consideration any accommodations or modifications needed on the job. In its simplest form, CAPS is a grid that consists of the following components:

- *Time/Activity*. This section indicates daily activities and the corresponding times, including arrival at work, breaks, lunch, meetings, the work task, and departure from work.
- *Skills to Learn*. These are tasks that must be mastered to be successful in the job. In addition, mode of instruction (i.e., colleague, web-based program) is included.
- *Structure/Modifications*. This can encompass a wide variety of supports, including checklists, timers, written instructions, and agendas.
- *Reinforcement*. Reinforcement, including self-reinforcement, is an important component of job success. For example, affirmation can improve self-concept and performance. *(Before Jose used affirmations, he needed to be reassured that he was doing a good job and would often ask. The affirmations were instituted so Jose could reinforce himself rather than asking the same questions each day, "Did I sort the mail right?," "May I take my break now?," and "I am going home, so can I have my paycheck now?")*
- *Sensory Strategies*. Sensory supports and strategies, including self-regulation plans, are listed in this CAPS area. Earplugs, headphones, paperclips to use as fidget items, and paper to doodle on during meetings are examples of sensory supports.

- *Communication/Social Skills*. This could be a hidden curriculum item of the day, such as using a *Hidden Curriculum On the Go* app (download from Apple® iTunes, iPhone, and iTouch Applications) on your iPhone, iPod, iPad, or other device. Other tools under the area of communication/social skills supports include reminders to review news on a site such as yahoo.com to inspire topics of conversation with coworkers, conversation-starter cards, and a list of talking points for a meeting.
- *Data Collection*. This encompasses gathering information on the Skills to Learn. Data can indicate (a) completion of a self-assessment, (b) observation by a colleague, (c) performance evaluation, and so forth. In most workplaces, this can be done as part of performance evaluations and training plans as well as praise or redirection from supervisors.
- *Generalization Plan*. Because individuals with ASD often have problems generalizing information across settings, this section of the CAPS was developed to ensure that generalization of skills occurs from setting to setting, from activity to activity, etc. For example, a conversation-starter card used during a break may also be used during lunch.

CAPS can be developed by the employee, a job coach, transition specialist, vocational rehabilitation staff member, or any combination of these individuals, and only the sections of CAPS that would be most beneficial to the employee are completed. Below is a glimpse at how Lilia handles this.

■ ■ ■

In addition to having a self-regulation plan, Lilia developed a CAPS to help ensure that she can perform optimally on the job. She has used this type of road map throughout high school and college, individualizing it to match the demands of the environment. Lilia's CAPS appears in Table 4.5. She does not need supports during all activities, but those listed on the CAPS are crucial to Lilia's success. For example, Lilia has difficulty scrolling on the computer because it creates a feeling of motion sickness. Therefore, accessing information in books rather than on computers results in less fatigue and greater productivity for her. Even though all of the tax accounting resources she needs are available online from the Internal Revenue Service, Lilia keeps paper copies in her office. She has told her supervisor that it is essential that she receive all documents in printed form. Her CAPS lists this support and reminds Lilia to request these materials, as needed.

Lilia is also not good at "small talk," polite conversational chit-chat like commenting about the weather or asking about the upcoming trip a client told her about the last time Lilia saw her. Yet, this is an essential skill when talking with clients. She has learned that clients value not only accounting skills, but also the accountant's ability to recall personal facts about them and to briefly discuss events or topics they might find mutually enjoyable. Lilia has developed strategies that she can use to ensure that this social necessity is met. For example, after meeting with a client, Lilia writes any personal information discussed (i.e., spouse's name, number of children, pet's name, favorite sports team, vacation plans) on that client's address card. She quickly reviews the card before she meets with the client the next time.

Table 4.5

Comprehensive Autism Planning System (CAPS) for Lilia

Time/ Activity	Skills to Learn	Structure/ Modifications	Reinforcement	Sensory Strategies	Communication Social Skills	Data Collection	Generalization Plan
Entry to work/ leave work	Small talk	Review yahoo news for conversation topics	Friendship	-------------	Personal conversation reminders	Two personal comments	Use at gym
Break(s)	-------------	-------------	More productive	Regulation plan	If someone wants to talk, nicely tell them that this is de-stressing time	Check stress level	At home
Work task	Keep current on tax code	Hard copies of materials	More productive	Regulation plan	-------------	Billable hours	-------------
Meetings (work or with clients)	Small talk; smooth interactions	Agenda	Ask admin asst for feedback after meeting	Regulation plan; tea/coffee	Review address card prior to meeting with clients	Ask admin asst for feedback	-------------
Lunch	Small talk	Review yahoo news for topics; recall personal details of colleagues	Friendship	Regulation plan, as needed	If stressed and someone wants to talk, nicely tell them that this is de-stressing time or say, "I've got to catch up on some work"	Self-reflection	Meetings with clients

58

Interpreting and Reacting to Social Demands

Most people with ASD are valued for their ability to perform their jobs well. However, many have difficulty negotiating the myriad ordinary interactions that occur in the workplace, particularly interpreting and reacting to the ongoing social hidden curriculum demands throughout the day.

Each interaction with another person is considered social, regardless of the topic. So, a simple situation where a coworker asks, "May I use your stapler?" is a social interaction. A major challenge for individuals with ASD is the social element of their interactions with others. Indeed, the construct of autism means the social aspects of these interactions are often hidden to them. Therefore, it is illogical to expect them to correctly interpret and react to what is hidden from them. In fact, it is hit-or-miss whether they respond appropriately in a given social interaction, since they have no built-in method for assigning meaning to social interactions.

Individuals on the autism spectrum typically need to intentionally learn how to correctly assign meaning to social interactions. This is not easy, however, as every social interaction is comprised of many elements besides the meaning of the actual words spoken. For example, the meaning of the words spoken depends on the context of the situation. Often, a literal translation is not what is intended by the speaker, as illustrated in the following interaction between Marco and Geoff.

■ ■ ■

In the break room of the taxicab company where they work, Marco asked Geoff if he knew how to get to a particular address. Marco had to pick up a client from a meeting at an unfamiliar location. Geoff replied, "Yes, I do" and went on to talk about something else. After a short time Marco tried again, this time asking, "So, Geoff, you know how to get there?" Again, Geoff confirmed that he knew how to get to the address, but still made no move to actually give Marco the directions. Finally, in exasperation, Marco said, "Well then, how about the email address? Maybe I can email the passenger and get some information that way!"

Trying to be helpful, Geoff told Marco it would probably work better if he called or texted the passenger rather than emailing him. Marco thought Geoff was a jerk and decided he had had it – many such odd encounters proved to Marco that Geoff was a loser and not worth his time. Geoff went away thinking he had been helpful to Marco and had no idea why, from that point on, Marco stopped talking to him in the break room.

■　■　■

Hidden curriculum item related to Geoff's situation ...

- When a person asks if you know directions, he expects you to give him the directions if you know them, not just to say yes or no.

Situations like this occur multiple times throughout the workday. The trouble is that the hidden curriculum of social interactions is based on the assumption that we all know the "rules." And based on this assumption, when hidden curriculum violations occur, negative intent is often attributed to the violator.

Most people violate hidden curriculum rules on occasion. Socially, while this may be awkward, the moment passes, and all is well as the ensuing interactions get back on track in accordance with the hidden curriculum. However, individuals with ASD tend to make many more social mistakes than others because they do not automatically understand the hidden curriculum. As a result, they are not always able to "get back on track" socially in the eyes of others, including coworkers.

While the occasional misread social communications and faulty responses by a neurotypical employee can be overlooked, the sheer volume of misread social communications and faulty responses by an employee with ASD has a negative cumulative effect over time. In fact, it often leads to employees with ASD losing their jobs.

The good news is that although hidden curriculum knowledge doesn't come naturally for individuals with ASD, such information can be learned over time, and with practice it becomes easier. That is, a person can learn to detect it by intentionally watching and practicing.

For example, a person could play detective during a community out-ing event such as grocery shopping or going to a movie by intentionally watching for examples of hidden curriculum (Endow, 2012).

In the example above, if Geoff had understood the hidden cur-riculum assumption that when asked if you know something, such as directions, the person asking expects you to give him the direc-tions if you have them, the outcome would have been positive rather than negative.

Table 4.6
Elements of Social Interactions, in Addition to the Actual Words Spoken

- Gestures
- Facial expressions
- Proximity
- Tone and volume of voice
- The context of the interaction
- Other people present or within earshot
- Attributes of communicative partner (coworker/supervisor, male/female, younger/older, more experienced/less experi-enced, friend/acquaintance)

Table 4.6 lists elements of social interactions that must be considered to successfully interact with others – in addition to the actual words spoken. For example, a person can gather clues to determine when social missteps are occurring. One body-language indica-tor that a mistake is being made is that "question mark look" people get on their faces: They scrunch their eyebrows to-gether and downward while moving their head slightly backward.

Another indicator of a social error is when people sigh and/or roll their eyes, sometimes just slightly and other times a bit more dramatically. Sometimes, conversation partners change the topic of conversation. If a conversation partner ends a conversation in the middle of an explanation and walks away, this is often an indicator that a social error has been committed.

If this happens it is best not to go after the person right then. Instead, when you have a moment, think about the interaction and see if you can figure out the social error that you may have made. Sometimes you will be able to figure it out, and at other times you may need to ask a trusted friend or coworker, perhaps during a break.

For many social errors, it is enough to just understand them to avoid the same error in the future. But occasionally, when you have made a significant error, you may need to repair this by saying you are sorry. It is helpful to get another person's advice if you are not sure what to do.

How to Avoid and Repair Social Missteps

- **Think ahead.** Because it is difficult to gauge when a social error has been committed, it may be helpful to have a few phrases on hand.

- **Say "sorry" quickly in a conversation** works even if you have not committed a social error. In fact, whether you have something to be sorry for or not, you will likely be perceived as a somewhat polite and considerate person for saying "sorry" during a conversation. Nevertheless, even though this strategy generally works well, it is best to use it sparingly, perhaps reserving it for situations where you are completely baffled as to why a person seems displeased. Overuse of the strategy can cause you to appear socially awkward and thus backfire.

- **Use good manners and make comments that show concern** for a conversation partner is not only appreciated but also leaves the conversation partner with a favorable impression.

- **Show concern for others.** It is nice to show concern for your conversation partner's well-being in other ways, such as asking if the light is too bright if a person is squinting (dim it if the person says yes) or making room for him to set his coffee cup down. People who show they are thinking of the well-being and comfort of others by treating them kindly get more passes when they make hidden curriculum mistakes due to the good-will they have generated with their conversation partner.

- **Remember to say something if you are part of a conversation.** One area where many stumble in social exchanges is when they are not sure of what to say or how to respond. Some simply default to not responding at all so as not to make a mistake. While the intention of avoiding a social mistake is well meant, the result of remaining silent in such situations is that others interpret the silence to mean the listener is not interested, is aloof or unfriendly, doesn't like the work she has been hired to do, and/or doesn't like the speaker. Regardless of the speaker's specific interpretation, a negative perception about the individual with ASD can result.

  Further complicating such situations is that by remaining silent because of uncertainty about what to say, discomfort will inevitably display itself through facial expressions and body language. Such discomfort observed by the speaker is taken as further evidence to support an already negative perception of the silent communication partner.

  To avoid situations like this, the person with ASD can learn to recognize when it is occurring. This takes a bit of practice, but once aware of the fact that you are not meant to be a silent partner when others are speaking, it becomes easier.
  - One rule of thumb is not to remain completely silent for more than a minute or so.
  - Another rule of thumb is that each topic of the conversation requires some sort of input by the listener. Use such phrases as:
    ◊ "That's interesting!"
    ◊ "Really?"
    ◊ "Okay."
    ◊ "Alright."
    ◊ "I'm with you on that!" (if you agree with the speaker)

- **Observe others in conversation to see what types of phrases they use.** Be aware that some phrases change over time. For example, popular phrases, such as "cool," "hip," "awesome," and "sweet," come into vogue for a certain length of time and are then replaced by the next "in" word or phrase. If you want to fit in with those around you, it is important to use in-vogue phrases. Also, it is best to choose from the words and phrases typically used by those in your workplace.

  In most workplace interactions with coworkers, a relaxed manner of speaking is accepted, such as "got it" in response to an understood explanation. But the landscape changes when your communication partner is a supervisor or boss. This relationship is more formal, so it is wise to convey this in conversation. For example, when asked if you understand, it is better to say, "I understand" than the more informal "got it." Using more formal language is a demonstration of respect for individuals who are in a position of authority. It is also wise to use this sort of language in meetings when the boss is present even though many coworkers are also in attendance. A good rule of thumb here is: *In any group situation, use the language suited to the person in the group with the highest position of power or authority.*

- **Do not use certain words and phrases repeatedly.** For example, it would seem rather odd if you said "okay" every few moments during a conversation. In fact, after using one of these words or phrases as your contribution to the conversation, you might want to add a more substantial comment or ask a question about the subject being discussed.

- **Use body language that shows you are interested.** When someone is uncomfortable and doesn't know what to say during a conversation, his body language portrays this. But people can intentionally change their body language. This is helpful during conversations as a means of showing interest.

  Some ways you can show interest by using body language include:

  – Smiling

- – Nodding (to indicate affirmation and agreement)
- – Looking at the person talking
- – Leaning slightly toward the person talking
- **Refrain from engaging in other tasks** such as texting, emailing, straightening up your work area, or doing anything else that diverts your attention away from your communication partner during a conversation.

Handling Criticism

■ ■ ■

Heinrich prided himself on having work projects done ahead of schedule and eagerly presented them to his boss. After several months of doing so, Heinrich was very surprised when, upon presenting him with the latest project, his boss told him that in the future he wanted Heinrich to hand in completed projects to the secretary. The boss went on to explain that several employees were working on various parts of the project. The secretary would collect the individual parts and then present them all to the boss on the project's due date.

Unfortunately, hearing this made Heinrich so upset that the boss's explanation did not even register with him. All Heinrich could think was that he wasn't doing anything wrong and wanted the boss to know it. He said, "I am doing what I've always done. I have always turned in my projects early to you and you tell me thanks each time. It's always worked out just fine. There is no reason to change it!"

The boss calmly reiterated his explanation, but Heinrich was too upset to follow it. He blurted, "You are such an idiot to change something that has been working just fine. Didn't you ever hear the saying 'Don't fix what ain't broken'? No wonder people can't stand your guts!" Heinrich then stormed out, throwing his file folder containing the work project in the boss's wastebasket on the way.

■ ■ ■

Even under the best circumstances, there inevitably comes a time when your boss or supervisor has to let you know that they would like you to do something differently or that you did something wrong and, therefore, have to do it over. Nobody likes these kinds of situations, and receiving this sort of information can trigger big emotions very quickly. Because their neurology does not automatically regulate emotion, individuals with ASD often have to do something intentionally to get their high emotional state to come down.

■ ■ ■

For example, Heinrich might have excused himself until he calmed down rather than spouting off to the boss. He could have gone for a short walk to get a soda from the vending machine, taken a break, or simply gone back to his office and closed the door while he regrouped by doing wall pushups. For Heinrich, all of these strategies had proven to be helpful to reduce emotional intensity in the past. Others who have difficulty regulating emotions will have other strategies that are helpful to them in bringing high emotions down to a lower intensity.

■ ■ ■

Whenever possible, do not to respond – either verbally or in written form (text, note, email, etc.) – until your too-big emotions have come down. It is very tempting to respond out of anger or hurt feelings. Many people become defensive about their way of doing things. Sometimes workers tell their boss off. At other times, they behave in a variety of other ways that they later regret.

Instead of responding out of your hurt feelings or anger, it is better to say something like, "Thanks for telling me this. Let me think about it and get back you." In fact, it is a good idea to have a statement like this ready ahead of time, so you are prepared when this kind of situation arises as it is difficult to "think on one's feet," especially in an emotional situation. Also, try to get some background information, what did you do wrong/incorrectly and how can you correct it/do it correctly in *the future?* Basically, you will need to know what you did wrong or what did not meet expectations, how you are to do it differently in the future and, if it is the sort of task that has a timeline for completion, when the changes are due.

■ ■ ■

If Heinrich would have done this, he could have avoided telling his boss off. Having the phrase "Thanks for telling me" ready – thought out and practiced ahead of time, if necessary – would have given Heinrich the time he needed to leave and regulate his emotions rather than responding the way he did.

■ ■ ■

However, in many situations, you are expected to respond on the spot, such as when you have just been told you need to change the way you are doing one of your job duties and the boss or supervisor is waiting for your response.

If you are unable to think straight in the moment, you might at least thank the boss for the feedback. Then, after you have had time to think about it, you might go back to confirm with the boss what you understand you are to do differently. This could be in an email, a memo, or in person.

■ ■ ■

In the above example, if Heinrich would have thanked the boss for informing him of the change in procedures and walked away, he could have followed up later with an email. Once his emotions had calmed and he had a chance to think about it, he might have sent a simple email saying something like, "Just a followup to let you know that I have turned over my completed part of the XYZ project to Ms. Jones, your secretary. I understand that in the future you want me to turn in completed projects to Ms. Jones rather than giving them directly to you. Please let me know if there is anything else I should be doing."

■ ■ ■

Most people find that if they give themselves a little space – usually some time not in the company of the person who delivered the unfavorable news – their emotions settle down. However, that doesn't always happen for those with ASD. If you are a person who needs to do more than wait an hour or so to regain your composure, you might find *The Incredible 5-Point Scale* (Buron & Curtis, 2012; Buron, Brown, Curtis, & King, 2012) helpful in bringing intense emotions to a more manageable level. Table 4.7 illustrates how such a scale may be used to deal with the emotions surrounding criticism at work.

Table 4.7
Emotional Response to Criticism at Work

Rating	Feels Like	Calming Strategy
5	Blow up	Leave work – can't trust myself not to say or do things that will get me in trouble.
4	Irate	Go to bathroom for privacy. Do wall push-ups. Slowly, methodically, count to 50.
3	Slow burn	Walk to break room taking slow, deep breaths.
2	Ruffled	I can handle this. Keep working while taking, slow, deep breaths.
1	Calm and composed	Say, "Thanks for telling me. I will do it that way."

Sabotage

On rare occasions, people around you may become upset about the attention you receive for your abilities and expertise and, as a result, work to undermine you in order to look better in the eyes of management. In extreme cases, these people may actively seek to bring about your dismissal. Another motivator for this kind of sabotage is when one person seeks to promote their work profile by making another person's work look bad.

Common forms of sabotage in the workplace include ...

- A coworker spreading unfounded rumors or lies about you to your colleagues or your managers
- A manager deliberately withholding information that is vital to the success of the task you have been assigned
- A coworker withholding instructions from you but reporting that they had been conveyed to you and understood by you
- Somebody altering or ruining work that you have done with the intent of making you look incompetent
- Being given the wrong time for an important meeting, causing you to arrive late or to miss the meeting and, therefore, look bad or negligent in the eyes of management

The first thing to do if you believe that you are being sabotaged is to confirm or disprove that belief. If you are just being paranoid and accuse someone of sabotaging you, you could irreversibly damage your working relationship with that person and hurt your career prospects. One way of uncovering sabotage is to discuss the matter in private with a supervisor or a trusted friend and ask them for their opinion of the situation. (Avoid using the word "sabotage" in such conversations with a supervisor.)

Also, understand that sabotage is not a personal attack against you. You just happen to be the target. The person who is undertaking the sabotage may be worried about her job, feel disrespected by fellow employees, or may simply be seeking recognition.

With the help of a supervisor, appeal to the coworker's values and find some common ground. Include her in your work and remark positively on her successes. This approach may not stop the sabotage behavior, but it will give you a more defensible position should the matter come to a head. If you maintain a positive composure and ensure that a supervisor is aware of the situation, you have a better chance of being included in disciplinary action if matters escalate. If you overhear others making comments about your work, it is best to speak privately to your supervisor about this. Table 4.8 lists additional suggestions for how to address sabotage in the workplace.

Table 4.8
Five Ways to Address Acts of Sabotage

1. Check with someone you trust to make sure you're not being paranoid and that it is truly an act of sabotage.
2. Figure out what might be driving the other person's behavior.
3. Ask for a meeting with the person, perhaps with the assistance of your supervisor.
4. Brainstorm how you can help the other person achieve her goals *and* meet your own needs.
5. Most important, don't let the other person's poor behavior jeopardize your own professionalism (Ferrell, 2010).

Remember that attempts to sabotage are generally rare. It is most likely that you have misread a situation. Asking for clarification from the person involved or a third party can be helpful.

Summary

Understanding and being able to perform the job task, while essential, is only the beginning in terms of a worker's ability to keep her job. For individuals with ASD, acting in accordance with the hidden curriculum of the workplace is often a much greater challenge, and one that can jeopardize their ability to keep their job if not handled appropriately.

But there is hope! Often, a person with ASD is able to better manage the social landscape of employment when he brings intentionality to the three major areas discussed in this chapter: (a) arriving at work ready to engage, (b) managing stress to maintain engagement throughout the workday, and (c) interpreting and reacting appropriately to social demands.

Chapter Five

Hidden Curriculum Items for the Workplace

Not all social mistakes are equal. That is, while you have some leeway when committing some mistakes, such as reaching for a stapler in a coworker's cubby without first asking permission to do so, other mistakes can have disastrous results. For example, some behaviors, even though they may be the result of social misunderstanding, are against the law such as forced sexual contact with a person who doesn't want it (rape) or taking money or items that do not belong to you (theft). A person who has difficulty with automatically understanding the hidden curriculum can memorize behaviors that are illegal and be diligent to avoid those behaviors at all costs.

Another category of serious social mistakes has to do with cultural taboos. For example, in the United States sexual misconduct and drug offenses are cultural taboos. This means that society has deemed these things to be so bad that we not only have laws against them but also very harsh consequences for behavior that falls into these categories. For example, a person might get arrested for shoplifting while out on his lunch break, but it may not affect his job. But if that person smoked pot or consumed some street drug during his lunch break, he could lose his job over it.

This chapter consists of a list of hidden curriculum items that impact various aspects of employment. For ease of navigation, items have been divided into categories. They are not intended to be exhaustive lists but the start of examples of the hidden curriculum pertaining to a given category topic. Some variation in the items may exist, depending on your place of employment. Check these items against your own experiences at work and with trusted friends or colleagues.

Also included in this chapter are suggested activities to enhance your understanding of the hidden curriculum as it relates to employment. Often, interacting with new ideas and knowledge allows us to better carry them out in our lives; in addition, it makes learning new things more fun. Please feel free to use the suggested activities in the ways that are most helpful to you.

General Rules

Before even stepping into your new workplace, you can begin to familiarize yourself with the hidden curriculum items you are likely to find there. Some of the general hidden curriculum rules you may have run into before, especially if you have already been in the workforce, either as a paid employee or as a volunteer. Other items may be totally new to you.

Hidden curriculum items related to general workplace behavior ...

- It is not a good policy to make personal calls at work unless it is an emergency.

- Never use a derogatory name about your boss when speaking to coworkers, even if they do. It can backfire and cause you problems, including possible loss of job.

- In most workplaces, it is not acceptable to do personal email, texting, or surfing the Internet for personal pleasure while at work. Find out the rule at your workplace and abide by it whether or not it is written in the employee handbook.

- When you go into your boss's or coworkers' offices, do not try to read what is up on their computer screen. What is on somebody's computer screen is usually considered private.

Hidden curriculum items related to general workplace behavior ...

- Coworkers generally don't ask one another to loan them large sums of money, but they may occasionally ask for a small loan, such as enough money to cover lunch. If you are asked for a large loan, it is wise to decline. Ask a trusted relative or friend if in doubt.

- People generally do not discuss their income with coworkers as this is considered confidential information.

- If a coworker gets a promotion, it is polite to congratulate her regardless of whether you think she deserved it.

- It is not a good idea to tell jokes at work having to do with race, sex, religion, or politics.

- In most workplaces, you will lose your job for displaying angry behavior. Yelling, swearing, and similar means of communication are unprofessional and typically not tolerated.

- Discussing personal problems is best done with a good friend or relative, not with a coworker.

✱ Suggested Activity

Sort the Category: After reading over the General Rules category of hidden curriculum items, go back and sort them in a way that makes sense to you. For example, you might ...

- "X" the items you already know and have no difficulty utilizing

- "!" the items that are new and novel ideas you have never considered before

- Mark "I" for Important. Choose the two or three items that you find the most important to remember. These may be items you find difficult or items that are new ideas, or perhaps something you are familiar with, but easily forget.

Note: You may put more than one mark by an item.

Dress and Grooming

The way you dress and groom yourself can be considered your first introduction to others because people will see you and take in that visual information about you before you have even had a chance to introduce yourself. Therefore, your grooming and manner of dressing are very important, whether you like it or not.

Some workplaces have certain grooming requirements; for example, in most areas of the food service industry, workers must wear hairnets or hats. In some places all hair must be off the shoulders, so if a worker has long hair it has to be put up into an off-the-shoulder style. Regardless of any grooming requirements, it is important for all employees, in whatever place of employment, to be clean and neatly groomed each day they go to work.

Besides good grooming, it is important to dress in a manner that is appropriate to your workplace. Some companies have a written policy on dress code standards. If so, be sure to abide by it. Others have no written policy but have informal standards. These standards may or may not be clearly spelled out to you, but still, as an employee you are meant to fit into these informal dress code standards. Therefore, it is important to figure out how you are meant to dress.

Hidden curriculum items related to dress and grooming ...

- Some people consider it fashionable to wear flannel pajama pants out in public. This practice is not right or wrong but simply a fashion trend. It is almost never appropriate in work settings.

- A good rule of thumb concerning professional attire in work settings is to show no visible cleavage or midriff.

- If for any reason you do not like washing your hands in public restrooms, carry and use a small bottle of hand sanitizer.

- If you are female and wish to fit in, it is important to know that in many cultures facial hair on females is not socially acceptable. There are a variety of ways to remove unwanted facial hair. Ask a trusted friend or family member if you need information or help doing this.

**Hidden curriculum items related to
dress and grooming ...**

- Before going to work, bathe and use deodorant so that you won't smell bad to others.

- Many kinds of jobs require you to wear a uniform. Some jobs require you to wear a hairnet, an ID card on a lanyard, or something else. If you absolutely cannot meet these requirements, ask a trusted friend or relative to help you figure out a good way to handle the situation.

- Do not wear an outfit that reveals any of your undergarments. This sort of attire is deemed unprofessional.

- If your workplace has "casual Fridays," it means that workers do not have to wear their usual work clothes on Fridays. It is important to find out exactly what kind of clothing is permissible to wear as different workplaces have different rules about this.

- People generally wear different clothing each day. If something you wear today, such as a sweater or a pair of pants, is still clean and can be worn another time before washing, it is best to wait a few days before wearing it to work again.

✱ Suggested Activities

Plan Grooming Time: Think through what you will need to do in order to arrive at your place of employment clean and well groomed. Will you take a shower in the morning or evening? How often do you need to wash your hair? Get a haircut? How long does it take to brush your teeth, style your hair, trim your nails, apply makeup (if you wear makeup), etc.? Make a list called Daily Grooming and write down each grooming task you need to do each day. Then, figure out how long these tasks usually take you. Add a few minutes to account for situations that may take a little longer. The total will be the time you need to set aside for grooming each day before going to work. If you have the time to groom set aside in your before-work routine, you can be confident that you won't be rushed and tempted to skip important grooming aspects. This will help ensure you arrive at work well groomed every day.

Learn the Dress Code: Determine the dress code for your place of employment. If you wear a uniform, this is easy! If not, you can look for a dress code policy, but more important, look at the other employees. What are they wearing? Are they formally dressed, as in wearing suits and dresses, dressed in jeans and tee shirts, or somewhere in between? Once you have determined the dress code, match up the clothes you own. Do you have the right kind of clothes for work? If you work five days in a row such as a Monday-through-Friday job, it might be convenient for you to own five days of work-appropriate changes of clothing. This will allow you not to have to worry about washing clothes during the work week.

Work Attendance and Calling in Sick

Although attendance at work is not taken like attendance in school settings, regular attendance is nevertheless very important and is definitely noticed! In fact, most workplaces have attendance policies. And past attendance is often a consideration when there is an opportunity for a promotion or a pay increase.

But even though attendance is important, there are times when you will not be able to go to work. The most common reason for this is sickness. Some workplaces give you a certain amount of sick days to use each year. All workplaces expect to be notified ahead of time when you are too ill to come to work.

Hidden curriculum items related to general workplace behavior ...

- Even if there is a snowstorm, your place of employment may remain open and you may be expected to work. If you cannot get to work due to dangerous weather conditions, you must call in to report it just as you do when you are sick.

- When you return to work after taking a sick day, people may ask how you are feeling. They are not asking for a detailed medical report. An answer such as "much better, thank you" is generally the expectation.

Hidden curriculum items related to general workplace behavior ...

- When returning to work after being ill, do not discuss the details of any bodily functions pertaining to your illness. This is considered by most to be too much information and rude.

- Part-time workers do not usually get the same paid holiday time off as full-time workers. If in doubt, it is better to ask than to simply not show up for work on a holiday if you work part time.

- When a coworker informs you that you cannot leave work early but must ask first, know that you are asking for permission and, therefore, must receive a "yes" answer in order to leave. If the answer is "no," you cannot leave even though you have asked.

- Even if you have a good reason for being late to work, know that most workplaces do not tolerate this behavior more than once or twice. Even if people are pleasant about it, you could lose your job over it.

- Time sheets in the workplace need to be completed in the prescribed manner, turned in on time, and given to the correct person if you expect to be paid on time.

✷ Suggested Activity

Calling in Sick: Locate the company policy for calling in sick. If you cannot be 100% sure you will remember this policy, make a copy of it to take home with you. When the day comes that you wake up too sick to go to work, you will need to know exactly what to do. Typically, there is a specific number to call or person to report your absence to. Additionally, many workplaces require a doctor's note if you are absent for more than a day or two. This is important to know so you can determine whether you need to see a doctor so as to have that note when returning to work.

Transportation

Once you have a job, you will need to get there! Most often this involves utilizing some sort of transportation. Just as with all other aspects of work and of life in general, it is important to understand the hidden curriculum involved with various modes of transportation. Whether you drive, ride with a coworker, or use public transportation, such as a bus, taxi, or train, you can be assured that each of these contexts includes its very own hidden curriculum! Discover and learn it, and you will have the opportunity to more comfortably fit into the time traveling to and from your workplace.

Hidden curriculum items related to transportation ...

- When finding a seat on a bus, it is expected that you will not sit next to a stranger if other seats are available.

- If you find yourself routinely accepting rides from a friend or co-worker, you should help pay for gas or show your appreciation by doing something nice in return, such as taking the person out for lunch or giving a small thank-you gift.

- If you carpool to work, know that even though it is a driver's legal responsibility to ensure that passengers wear seat belts, it is unnecessary to announce this fact as most people know it. A friendly "buckle up" is usually sufficient.

- When driving alone in your car, it is fine to sing along with the radio or CD player. However, know that most people do not do this when others are in the car unless everybody agrees to sing along.

- If a coworker gives you a ride to or from work on a stormy day, don't expect that person to give you a ride every time the weather is bad. If you want a ride, ask the person if you might pay her to pick you up and take you home on bad-weather days.

✽ Suggested Activity

"X" the items above that apply to the type of transportation you use to get to and from your job. Then, think of additional hidden curriculum items and add them to this list. If you have difficulty thinking of items, ask a trusted friend or relative. For example, you might ask your brother, "I am carpooling to work. What do people generally know about how carpooling works?"

The Work Environment

This category has an unlimited number of rules! Some hidden curriculum rules are common across workplaces, such as treating others with respect and dignity, but many rules of the work environment vary from one workplace to the next. In the following list you may find few or many rules that apply in your work environment.

Hidden curriculum items related to the work environment ...

- After walking into an elevator, turn around to face the door so you are ready to exit when you get to your floor.

- Elevators are designed so that the largest crowd they can accommodate will not exceed the weight capacity. It is not polite to say to a person that she has caused the total weight to be over the posted capacity, even if you believe it is true.

- It is an unwritten rule in the United States to walk on the right-hand side of a staircase, even if you are left-handed and would rather use the left-hand rail. Only use the left side if nobody else is using the staircase.

- Sometimes stalls in public restrooms are out of toilet paper. It is wise to check upon entering, especially if you are not carrying a tissue that might be used instead.

- If you splash a lot of water on the counter top while washing your hands, it is considerate to wipe up after yourself.

- Do not rearrange a coworker's workspace. Even if a coworker is messy, it is not your business to tell him or to rearrange his workspace.

- When there is a fire drill at your workplace, you are expected to immediately exit the building. If you are not sure what to do, simply follow the other workers.

✱ *Suggested Activity*

My Work Environment Rules: Try to figure out the rules so that you can avoid embarrassment when you violate a rule just because you didn't know it ahead of time. To do so, first look over the items below. Mark each item that applies to your particular work environment. Then, think of the other hidden, not-so-obvious "rules." For example, in one workplace it was okay for workers to help themselves from the supply closet when they ran out of supplies, but it was not okay for them to take an entire box of copy paper to the copy machine on their wing of the building. Instead, they were to take only one or two reams of paper at a time.

It is okay if you can't think of any rules right away. Just be on the lookout for them, and before long you will start to discover them. One way to detect them is to watch how the other workers act. What sort of hidden rules do they follow? Another way is to pay attention to key phrases that are a signal for "here comes a hidden curriculum rule." These key phrases are:

"I shouldn't have to tell you, but …"

"It should be obvious that …"

"Everyone knows …"

"Common sense tells us …"

"No one ever …" (Myles et al., 2013, p. 5)

The Job Task

Most people can learn to perform the tasks required for their jobs quite well. The difficulty is that embedded in the job tasks are social expectations that employees will more or less automatically learn. When you are new on the job, you are given leeway because it is expected that it will take time for new employees to "learn the ropes." ("Learn the ropes" is an expression meaning to learn the hidden curriculum of the situation, in this case of the job tasks.)

Because the expectation is that new employees won't know the hidden curriculum, but will learn it in a short time, you can use this to your advantage during the first few weeks of your job. For example, you might ask directly for the information by saying to a fellow employee something like, "So, give me the scoop on what I need to know for the team meeting." You might do this when you are encountering a new job-related task for the first few times, but after you have done the task several times, in this case attending team meetings, you would not be able to directly solicit this information without appearing awkward.

Hidden curriculum items related to the job task ...

- "The customer is always right" is not a fact. It is a phrase businesses use to remind workers not to argue with customers, but to act toward them as if they are right. This is considered a good business practice.

- In some workplaces, workers are expected to take unfinished work home to complete it. In other workplaces, this is not expected. Know the expectation in your workplace and follow it.

- While at a work meeting, only talk about the subject being discussed, and only do so when you have something to say that hasn't already been brought up. Also, it's considered rude to have side conversations with the person next to you while the meeting is going on.

- When at a work meeting, never make negative comments such as "how stupid" or "what an idiot" when someone says something you don't agree with.

- Even if a coworker offers what you consider a stupid idea during a meeting, don't say so or point out why the idea is stupid. If you have a better idea, you might instead say something like, "Another suggestion is ..."

- If you are unable to hear what someone is saying in a meeting, politely tell the person and ask him to repeat it.

- During a meeting at work, it is better to offer your own ideas than to cut down someone else's. No matter how stupid you think somebody's ideas are, it is better not to say so.

✳ *Suggested Activity*

During the first month of a new job, or whenever you are given new job tasks, think through your daily work schedule and choose a time when you might use the above strategy. In addition, try to figure out which coworker you might engage to help you. It is important to use this strategy sparingly, maybe once a day at most, and to use it with different people over time so that you are not posing the same question to the same person each day as new job tasks arise.

Workplace Communication

Communication in the workplace can be difficult, especially if you are a literal thinker. Rarely is everyday communication literal. That means if you respond based on your literal understanding of what another person has said, your response, in all likelihood, will be inappropriate.

Hidden curriculum items related to workplace communication ...

- When somebody says, "I'm not even going to answer that question," it likely means that you made a social misstep by asking the question in the first place. Apologize and later ask a trusted friend if you need somebody to explain the situation.

- It is a social mistake called "bragging" if you talk on and on about your talents and abilities. However, it is okay to allow someone else to talk on and on about your abilities as long as you don't join in.

- When someone addresses you by name, be sure to acknowledge them. If you don't look at them or respond verbally, they won't know if you heard them.

- When having a conversation, you are interrupting if you start talking before another person has finished what she was saying. It is better to wait and make sure the other person is finished than to interrupt.

- It is considered impolite to monopolize a conversation. To avoid monopolizing a conversation, keep in mind that your turn should take approximately as long as other people's turns.

Hidden curriculum items related to workplace communication ...

- When people need to move past you and say, "Excuse me," you do not have a choice about whether or not to excuse their actions. Consider these words a polite warning that your space is about to be invaded.

- Most people use absolute speech incorrectly, such as saying someone is *never* happy or is *always* bossy. Even though these absolute statements are rarely correct, it is not a good idea to point it out. If you wish, assign a correct translation silently.

- It is considered rude to start talking with someone who is on the phone. If you start talking to someone and then realize she is on the phone, simply say "sorry" and stop talking.

- It is courteous to remove your headphones or ear buds when someone comes up and starts talking to you even if you can still hear them.

- Even though it may be the truth, it is generally unacceptable to tell another adult that she is acting inappropriately.

- It is not appropriate for you to tell a coworker when he is doing his job poorly. This is the boss's responsibility.

- When a coworker gets an award or a special recognition, congratulate her even if you think she didn't deserve it. It is best to keep such opinions to yourself.

- If you are upset over something that happened at work, it is better to say you would like to discuss it later than to say something you may end up wishing you hadn't said.

- At work you may have to wait, sometimes for several days, to get your question answered. If waiting is difficult for you, it is better to ask when you can expect to receive an answer than asking the same question again and again.

- It is generally not a good idea to swear at work, even if other workers do so. It is too easy to swear in front of the wrong person (your boss or somebody who is opposed to swearing) or at the wrong time. Doing so could adversely affect your job.

- If you are asked if you know the directions to a certain place or if you have a certain item such as a stapler, screw driver, or tape, even though the real answer is "yes" or "no," what people generally want are the directions or the item rather than a yes or no answer.

✱ Suggested Activity

Pause and Match: If you tend to make sense out of language through a literal filter, the following will likely save you from miscommunication and from social embarrassment! The strategy is fairly simple: Intentionally pause before responding to others in your workplace to give yourself a moment to determine if your literal interpretation of the conversation matches the topic of the conversation (Endow, 2012).

Strange Things People May Say

Sometimes people laugh when somebody makes a hidden curriculum mistake because it is funny. This is okay. Laughing that arises due to misunderstood hidden curriculum is rarely the sort of laughing that means people are bullying. One nice thing about this kind of laughter is that you can join in.

Hidden curriculum items related to strange things people may say ...

- If anyone says you are "out of line," it means that whatever you did or said is unacceptable. It is generally best to apologize immediately, and then as soon as possible afterwards ask a trusted friend to explain if you do not understand the situation. This is especially important in the workplace, as being out of line can lead to being fired.

- "TMI" stands for "too much information." When people respond to you by saying "TMI," it means you are divulging too much information either in quantity or in detail.

- If a coworker asks what you are going to do during the weekend, he is generally referring to entertainment or special events, not to the usual household cleaning, washing clothes, and running errands. If you have no special activity planned, it is appropriate to say, "Not much. What are you doing?"

Hidden curriculum items related to strange things people may say ...

- A "roast and toast" is a retirement party where the guest of honor is made fun of in a teasing, non-hurtful manner by fellow coworkers who wish to share stories or memories about her. If you have a story to tell, it might be wise to run it by a trusted friend before sharing it with the crowd, especially if you are not sure if it is a good story to tell.

- When coworkers are complaining and someone sarcastically makes the comment "Go tell the boss about that," it means that it is highly unlikely that circumstances will change. It does not mean that anyone should really tell the boss.

- If your boss invites everyone to "brainstorm," she is inviting workers to share all ideas that come to mind without evaluating the merit of each idea. Don't offer comments evaluating the ideas others come up with during a brainstorming session.

- If someone says he is "playing devil's advocate," he means that he is taking a position he may not necessarily believe himself but is taking an opposing view so others might think of all possibilities of the subject they are discussing.

- If a coworker says he is "down to the wire," it means he is really close to the time of the absolute deadline to turn in his work. Therefore, don't speak to him or in any way distract him from meeting his deadline.

- If someone says he got his "walking papers," it means he got fired.

- If a coworker tells you something "off the record," she intends that you will not attribute to her whatever it is she is telling you. It is best simply to not repeat anything told to you "off the record."

✱ *Suggested Activity*

Laugh Along: "If somebody starts laughing, I immediately laugh along. Most times I don't understand why I am laughing. Luckily, it usually doesn't matter because most people like to laugh with you. Funny thing is that the other person usually makes enough of a comment that I come to understand why we are both laughing. If not, I can usually figure it out later, or if I trust the person enough I can let him or her in on the secret that I don't have a clue why we are laughing. Then, once the situation has been explained, we both have a really good laugh together!" (Endow, 2012, pp. 51-52).

Breaks and Lunchtime

For those who do not have a neurology that allows them to understand the hidden curriculum automatically, unstructured time during the workday is typically the most difficult period of the day. Break time and lunchtime are usually the hardest time because they are the most socially demanding. Besides that, the employment-related knowledge that can get you by in the job environment often does not matter in the lunchroom or break room.

■ ■ ■

For example, Joe often felt embarrassed and self-conscious because he did not understand the bantering camaraderie and teasing remarks his coworkers engaged in during the lunch break. He enjoyed the guys he ate with but didn't always know when they were handing out helpful information versus when they were teasing such as, "You dance those invoices over to the big boss as soon as you get them." In this case, the important information is that the boss expects to receive invoices as soon as possible. The teasing part is that workers are not expected to literally dance when delivering the invoices. Joe's coworkers didn't quite know what to make of him, and Joe was afraid they would decide he wasn't part of the group because he didn't always understand their teasing ways.

Joe decided to use partial disclosure – telling enough information to be helpful in a particular situation rather than giving a full disclosure of his diagnosis and what it means. Joe said, "Hey guys, got something important to say here. Don't know if you figured it out by now, but I have a disability. It makes it tough for me to sort out the meaning of words. My brain can't always sort out the teasing from the real. I worry that if my brain betrays me, I might get in trouble. Like what if I really danced those invoices over to Greg's office? So, please clue me in if I am going the wrong way, and when I'm not sure of something, I will just ask if it is time to dance."

Joe's coworkers appreciated his disclosure. From that point on, they kept Joe clued in by saying, 'it's not a dance, dude" or "sit this dance out" whenever Joe looked puzzled over their teasing ways. And when things were not a joke but something Joe needed to really do, they would tell him, "this one is real, dude" or "we are playing your song," both comments that Joe understood. Likewise, whenever Joe was confused, he would ask, "dancing shoes?" and the guys would steer him in the right direction.

■ ■ ■

Hidden curriculum items related to breaks and lunchtime ...

- In some workplaces, you may use the restroom whenever you please. In other workplaces, you are expected to use the restroom only during your breaks and in cases of emergency. Ask a coworker if you do not know the expectation at your workplace.

- When entering the lunchroom or break room at work, you may find people laughing. Their laughter likely has to do with the conversation they're having and not with you.

- If you are involved in a lunch meeting at work, remember not to talk while you have food in your mouth. If it is difficult for you to focus during the meeting, eat beforehand and then just have something to drink during the meeting.

Hidden curriculum items related to breaks and lunchtime ...

- When a coworker brings a treat to work such as cookies or donuts, take only one serving at first. Later, if you are offered a second serving, it is fine to say "thanks" and accept it, if you wish.

- At some workplaces, an employee's lunchtime is a very specific time, for example, 11:30-12:00. At other workplaces, workers take a half hour for lunch, but the exact starting and stopping time is more flexible. It is important to know and follow the expectation at your workplace.

- If a coworker brings something for lunch that you personally would never eat, it is best not to say so or make any negative comments about the food.

- Work lunch breaks start from the time you leave your workspace, not from the time you begin eating your food.

- If you see that your friend or coworker has food between his teeth or on his face, do not announce it in front of others. You may tell him quietly if you wish. People usually become embarrassed if you announce this, but are often grateful if you tell them quietly.

- If your boss has told a coworker not to do something, such as eating at his computer, it likely means that other workers, including you, shouldn't do so either.

✹ Suggested Activity

Disclosure: If lunchtime and break time are especially difficult for you because of the social demands and if you often stick out as "odd" or "different," you might consider disclosure. Most of the time, you do not need to explain your disability; instead, explain how it affects you and what your coworkers could do to help you.

Relationships With Colleagues at Work and Socially

It is important to learn all you can about your new job, including how to get along socially with coworkers/colleagues in your workplace. One thing that is helpful to know is that there are social rules about who you can talk to about which topic. While it is easy to learn a rule such as, "Do not talk about sex or politics in the workplace," it is not so easy to learn the more subtle social rules. If you have difficulty in this area, you might find the following activity helpful.

Hidden curriculum items related to relationships with colleagues at work and socially ...

- We cannot depend on others at our places of employment or else-where to respond to our social missteps in the same way our trusted friends do. Even though you can depend on your friends when they are with you, they will not always be with you, such as when you are working, doing errands, and generally living your life.

- If you disagree with something somebody is saying, you may politely state so one time, but to go on and on about your point of view would be rude.

- If you see a coworker or your boss in a public place such as at the grocery store or the gym, it doesn't mean they want to be social with you. It is best to greet them in a friendly way and only enter into a conversation if they start one.

- When you are finished speaking with a coworker or friend, even though it is literally true, don't say, "I am done with you." This sounds impolite to most people in this situation, as the common meaning of the phrase is that you no longer want to have anything to do with the person.

- It is okay if you don't like all of your coworkers. Just treat them respectfully. Also, don't mention to others in your workplace which coworkers you like and which ones you don't like.

- If a coworker consistently does something that bothers you and it is negatively impacting your work, try to resolve it by explaining to your colleague how his actions are adversely affecting your work and asking him to help you by changing whatever he is doing, if possible.

Hidden curriculum items related to relationships with colleagues at work and socially ...

- If two coworkers are talking together very quietly, they may be having a private conversation. Unless it is an emergency, wait until another time to approach them.

- If you are having a gathering at your home for some of your co-workers who also happen to be your friends, don't talk about it in front of coworkers who have not been invited.

- If you overhear coworkers talking about going out after work or on weekends, don't invite yourself along. If you are not invited, do not go.

- While the boss is on vacation, another employee may be appointed as the "go-to" person for any workers who have questions. Treat this person with the same respect you treat your boss, no matter what you think of the employee.

- If your boss or a coworker is unhappy with something you have done and is discussing it with you, don't start talking about a totally different subject. If you do, she may think you are not taking her seriously. If appropriate, make plans for how you might remedy the situation.

- If you are asked to lie for someone and you would rather not, you might say something like, "I won't volunteer anything, but if I am asked, you need to know I am not good at covering up the truth."

✱ Suggested Activity

Using a piece of paper, make three columns as in the example below. Ask a trusted relative, friend, or job coach to help you fill in the columns. As situations arise at work where people react to your topic of conversation by changing the subject abruptly, walking away, or otherwise not responding, add the topic of conversation to your list to review with your trusted friend, relative, or job coach. This can help you to determine if it was the topic of your conversation or something else that was problematic. Feel free to copy and use this table, adding as many boxes as you need.

Note: Many people, especially those who tend to be visual thinkers, find that having a visual like this helps them to avoid making mistakes because it shows where to put which words. Some people have reported that after using this kind of sorting list, the list pops up in their head before they start talking about a new topic. When they see the list, they can pretty accurately guess which column to put their words in before actually saying them. Thus, the visual gives them a way to consider their words before actually saying them.

Okay to Say at Work	Safe to Say With Non-Work Friends and Family	Notes
Great football game Sunday!		Part of greeting or topic at break or lunch.
	I liked the special music at my church last Sunday.	The topic of religion is best not discussed at work.
I was so sick yesterday.	I threw up six times yesterday.	Employers/coworkers do not need details on your illness. Your family and friends might not want more detail either, but it is not prohibited.

Relationships With Supervisors/Bosses

Relationships with supervisors and bosses are among the most difficult relationships to socially negotiate. A large part of the problem seems to hinge on the fact that supervisors and bosses are generally friendly in the way they talk to workers. Because their words are friendly, it is hard to remember that supervisors and bosses, even though they are friendly, are not your friends and, therefore, cannot be treated as such. Often friendly sounding words from a supervisor or boss have a totally different social meaning than if a coworker said the same words.

Hidden curriculum items related to relationships with supervisors/bosses ...

- It usually doesn't work well to tell your boss that something isn't fair. This is a comment a disgruntled child would make and thus, you run the risk of appearing childish and/or argumentative if you tell your boss that something is unfair.

- When your boss makes a mistake, it's not a good idea to tell him he screwed up, even if it's the truth. This warning is even more relevant when other colleagues are present.

- If your boss asks if you have any questions, her intent is that you ask questions pertaining to the topic or project she is discussing. You are not to ask about something totally irrelevant to her intent or to the topic.

- When your boss asks you to do something, the implication is that you *will* do it. Rarely is it up to you to decide whether or not you will follow through with what your boss is asking you to do.

- When your boss is busy or unhappy, this is not a good time to ask questions unless they pertain to an emergency.

- No matter how convinced you become that your boss or a worker who is your superior is not smart, do not share this information with him or others, even if your intent is to be helpful to the company.

- Bosses usually give work directions to employees. When an employee doesn't follow the work directions, he risks getting reprimanded. If it happens repeatedly, he may get fired.

- If another employee is in the boss's office, it is best to wait until she leaves before you go in to ask a question or discuss a business concern.

- It is fine to think your boss is boring, but never tell her so.

- If your boss indicated she will be with you in a moment and asked you to wait in her office, do not sit behind the desk in her chair.

- It is never okay to tell your boss to go to hell or to make any other rude comment to him when you don't like what he is telling you.

- In some workplaces, employees call the bosses by their first names. In other workplaces, calling a boss by her first name would be inappropriate. Paying attention to how other workers address the boss can help you figure out what to do.

Hidden curriculum items related to relationships with supervisors/bosses ...

- If your boss asks to use the copy machine even if you are in the middle of making lots of copies, the expectation is not only that you will let him but that you will act pleasant about it, no matter what you think or feel. Besides, it would be a good idea to offer to make the copies for him.

- If you get a new boss, she may do things differently than your old boss. Unless the new boss specifically asks how the former boss did something, don't offer this type of information.

- If your boss congratulates you on a job well done, simply say, "Thank you." Don't talk about how much you deserved it or how clever you were to figure out the project.

✽ Suggested Activity

The Hidden Meaning of What the Boss Says: Keep a running list of friendly sounding things your boss says to you. If something is puzzling to you, put a star next to it. You can make this list when you are away from work or on your own time at work, such as break time if you take breaks alone. (Note: This is not a good idea to do in front of coworkers in the break room when the expectation is that you will socialize with coworkers during break time.) Later, when you have an opportunity, you can discuss these things with a trusted relative, friend, counselor, or your job coach. Feel free to copy this table and add to it as many boxes as you need.

Friendly Things My Boss Says	Purely Friendly Comment	Comment With Hidden Meaning	Hidden Meaning
When you have time, please ...		X	You have no choice but to do whatever you are asked.
Good morning.	X		
It would be great if you could ...		X	This is usually a directive, meaning you will do whatever it is.

Company-Related Social Events

Company-related events can be social troublespots for employees who have difficulty picking up on hidden social meanings and expectations. Therefore, it is especially wise to discuss any out-of-the-ordinary event that is to happen in your workplace. Such events are generally announced in staff meetings, via email as invitations or announcements, posted on a bulletin board, or included in the company newsletter. Sometimes they are clearly marked as social events, but most times they are not.

Hidden curriculum items related to company-related social events ...

- Even though it is sometimes considered socially acceptable to curse, it is best not to do so unless you are absolutely sure that you won't offend anybody. Even then, it may be wise to wait until others have cursed first and see what happens.

- At a retirement party, attendees usually say favorable things about the retiree. Don't tell stories that will put the retiree in an unfavorable light.

- If names are drawn for a holiday gift exchange, it means that you only bring a gift for the person whose name you drew.

- If most of the workers are decorating their workspaces for the holidays, it may be one of those technically optional but socially mandatory workplace customs. If in doubt, it is likely best to go along with it and decorate your workspace, too.

- A holiday gift exchange in the workplace is usually optional. However, if every person is participating, it is likely an expectation that is technically optional, but socially required.

- If your workplace has a holiday project, such as collecting gifts for the homeless or contributing to a food drive, it is likely a mandatory social obligation for workers to participate. That is, the social repercussions of not doing as expected exceed the benefits of noncompliance.

**Hidden curriculum items related to
company-related social events ...**

- When going to a company picnic, you likely can bring your family or one close friend. If you are unsure, ask before bringing guests.

- If you attend a work-related function where alcohol is served, be mindful not to drink enough to lower your inhibitions. When you have had too much to drink, you may do and say things you will not be happy about once you are back to work.

- If you are asked to chip in for a gift for your boss, even if you would rather not, this is one of those mandatory social obligations in which it is in your own best interest to participate. Do so without any negative comments. It's best to act pleasant about it!

✱ Suggested Activity

Become a Social Events Detective in Your Workplace: Look for these events in the places/formats listed above. Your workplace may also have other ways to let employees know about these sorts of events. Each time you encounter one of these events, it is important for you to learn the hidden meanings. There are many ways in which you can do so. You can watch and ask to see what others are saying and doing, you can bring up the topic at break or lunchtime to see what others say about it, or you can discuss it with a friend, family member, or job coach. The important thing is to figure out which events are "socially mandatory" and the expected employee response or behavior surrounding them.

Avoiding Sexual Harassment

Something that confuses many individuals who have trouble learning the hidden curriculum is the topic of sexual harassment in the workplace. The legal definition of sexual harassment is "**unwelcome** verbal, visual, or physical **conduct of a sexual nature** that is **severe or pervasive** and **affects working conditions or creates a hostile work environment**" (http://www.equalrights.org/publications/kyr/shwork.asp). Each of these bolded words is further defined at the web site, which also contains a wealth of information about sexual harassment in the workplace.

Sexual harassment is difficult to understand because behaviors can mean different things to different people. One worker might tell another worker she looks pretty. It may be a compliment if said once. However, if said repeatedly, even if the giver is intending a compliment, the receiver would likely perceive it as harassment. The following is a short list of hidden curriculum items intended to help you avoid being in a situation involving sexual harassment.

Hidden curriculum items related to avoiding sexual harassment ...

- If you tell a coworker she looks hot, it can be perceived as a sexually harassing remark.

- Do not make remarks about the private parts of people's bodies, especially at work. It could be considered sexual harassment.

- It is socially acceptable for women to converse with one another in public restrooms. However, men typically do not speak to each other in that setting. Follow the rule for your gender.

✱ *Suggested Activity*

Attend a Workshop: Many workplaces offer workshops or inservice meetings on the topic of sexual harassment. If one is offered at your workplace, whether or not you are required to attend, take this opportunity to learn more about this topic by attending.

Avoid Giving Compliments Concerning Appearance: If you have trouble understanding where the line is between giving compliments and sexually harassing a coworker, it is best to refrain from giving any compliment on appearance. You could instead give compliments on other areas, such as when the coworker performs a job task well or does something thoughtful such as helping another worker.

Summary

Every work week is filled with the hidden curriculum in many social encounters. And every exchange that involves another person is a social encounter! As you broaden your awareness of the hidden curriculum in the workplace, you will become more comfortable and won't keep making the same social mistakes again and again.

Learning the items in this chapter is a starting point. Use it as a springboard for watching and discovering the hidden curriculum in your workplace. The more you learn to identify the hidden curriculum, the less it will be hidden from you. When that happens, employees with autism and other social challenges tend to fit in better and consequently have a more enjoyable and productive experience when they are at work.

References

Bakshy, E., Marlow, C., Rosenn, I., & Adamic, L. (n.d.). *The role of social networks in information diffusion. Informally published manuscript.* Available from eptint afXiv (1201.4145). Retrieved from http://www.scribd.com/facebook/d/78445521-Role-of-Social-Networks-in-Information-Diffusion

Buron, K. D., & Curtis, M. (2012). *The incredible 5-point scale: The significantly improved and expanded second edition: Assisting students in understanding social interactions and controlling their emotional responses.* Shawnee Mission, KS: AAPC Publishing.

Buron, K., Thierfeld Brown, J., Curtis, M., & King, L. (2012). *Social behavior and self-management – 5-point scales for adolescents and adults.* Shawnee Mission, KS: AAPC Publishing.

Cornbleth, C. (2011, February 22). *School curriculum: Hidden curriculum.* Retrieved from http://education.stateuniversity.com/pages/1899/Curriculum-School-HIDDEN-CURRICULUM.html

Dew, D. W., & Alan, G. M. (Eds.). (2007). *Rehabilitation of individuals with autism spectrum disorders* (Institute on Rehabilitation Issues Monograph No. 32). Washington, DC: The George Washington University, Center for Rehabilitation Counseling Research and Education

Endow, J. (2011). *Practical solutions for stabilizing students with classic autism to be ready to learn: Getting to go.* Shawnee Mission, KS: AAPC Publishing.

Endow, J. (2012). *Learning the hidden curriculum: The odyssey of one autistic adult*. Future Horizons.

Ferrell, R. (2010, October 13). *Are you being sabotaged at work?* Retrieved from http://msn.careerbuilder.com/Article/MSN-2434-Workplace-Issues-Are-You-Being-Sabotaged-at-Work/

Grandin, T., & Duffy, K. (2008). *Developing talents for individuals with Asperger syndrome and high-functioning autism – Updated,* Future Horizons.

Hagner, D., & Cooney, B. F. (2005). "I do that for everybody": Supervising employees with autism. *Focus on Autism and Other Developmental Disabilities, 20*(2), 91-97.

Henry, S. A., & Myles, B. S. (2007). *The Comprehensive Autism Planning Systems (CAPS) for individuals with Asperger Syndrome, autism and related disabilities: Integrating best practices throughout the student's day.* Future Horizons.

Howlin, P., Alcock, J., & Burkin, C. (2005). An 8-year follow-up of a specialist employment service for high-ability adults with autism and Asperger syndrome. *Autism, 9*(5), 533-549.

Hurlbutt, K., & Chalmers, L. (2004). Employment and adults with Asperger syndrome. *Focus on Autism and Other Developmental Disabilities,19*(4), 215-222.

Jackson, P. (1968). *Life in classrooms.* New York, NY: Holt, Rinehart, & Winston.

Kanpol, B. (1989). Do we dare teach some truths? An argument for teaching more "hidden curriculum." *College Student Journal, 23,* 214-217.

Kelly, R. (2009, August 09). [*Web log message*]. Retrieved from http://www.pearanalytics.com/blog/2009/twitter-study-reveals-interesting-results-40-percent-pointless babble.

Landmark, L. J., Ju, S., & Zhang, D. (2010). Substantiated best practices in transition: Fifteen plus years later. *Career Development for Exceptional Individuals, 33,* 165-176.

LaVoie, R. (1994). Learning disabilities and social skills with Richard LaVoie. In J. Bieber (Ed.), *Last one picked ... first one picked on.* Washington, DC: Public Broadcasting Service.

Müller, E., Schuler, A., Burton, B. A., & Yates, G. B. (2003). Vocational supports for individuals with Asperger Syndrome: Meeting the vocational support needs of individuals with Asperger Syndrome and other autism spectrum disorders. *Journal of Vocational Rehabilitation, 18*(3), 163-175.

Myles, B. S., Trautman, M. L., & Schelvan, R. L. (2013). *The hidden curriculum for understanding unstated rules in social situations for adolescents and young adults (2nd ed.).* Future Horizons.

Polimeni, M. A., Richdale, A. L., & Francis, A.J.P. (2005). A survey of sleep problems in autism, Asperger's disorder and typically developing children. *Journal of Intellectual Disability Research, 49,* 260-268.

Rzepecka, H., McKenzie, K., McClure, I., & Murphy, S. (2011). Sleep, anxiety, and challenging behavior in children with intellectual disability and/or autism spectrum disorders. *Research in Developmental Disabilities, 32,* 2758-2766.

Schutte, J. (2009, June 5). *Employment supports for individuals with autism spectrum disorders.* Retrieved from http://aheadd.org/blog/employment-supports-for-indivdiuals-autism-spectrum-disorders.

Vermeulen, P. (2012). *Autism as context blindness.* Future Horizons.

Wehmeyer, M. L., Gragoudas, S., & Shogren, K. A. (2006). Self-determination, student involvement, and leadership development. In P. Wehman (Ed.), *Life beyond the classroom: Transition strategies for young people with disabilities* (4th ed., pp. 41-69). Baltimore, MD: Paul H. Brookes.

Welcome to Future Horizon's Exclusive Hidden Curriculum Series

The Hidden Curriculum for Understanding Unstated Rules in Social Situations for Adolescents and Young Adults (Rev. ed.)

Brenda Smith Myles, PhD, Melissa L. Trautman, MsEd, and Ronda L. Schelvan, MsEd

ISBN: 9781937473747

The Hidden Curriculum and Other Everyday Challenges for Elementary-Age Children With High-Functioning Autism (Rev. ed.)

Haley Myles and Annellise Kolar

ISBN: 9781937473105

For more information and to order, go to www.fhautism.com

The Hidden Curriculum of Getting and Keeping a Job: Navigating the Social Landscape of Employment

Brenda Smith, Myles, PhD, Judy Endow, MSW, and Malcolm Mayfield, BS Civil Eng

ISBN: 9781937473020

Learning the Hidden Curriculum: The Odyssey of One Autistic Adult

Judy Endow, MSW

ISBN: 9781934575932

For more information and to order, go to www.fhautism.com

About the Authors:

Brenda Smith Myles, PhD, a consultant with the Ohio Center for Autism and Low Incidence (OCALI), the Ziggurat Group, and the Education and Treatment Services Project for Military Dependent Children with Autism, is the recipient of the Autism Society of America's Outstanding Professional Award, the Princeton Fellowship Award, and the Council for Exceptional Children, Division on Developmental Disabilities Burton Blatt Humanitarian Award. Myles has made over 500 presentations all over the world and written more than 150 articles and books on ASD. In addition, she served as the co-chair of the National ASD Teacher Standards Committee; was on the National Institute of Mental Health's Interagency Autism Coordinating Committee's Strategic Planning Consortium; collaborated with the National Professional Center on Autism Spectrum Disorders, National Autism Center, and the Centers for Medicare and Medicaid Services to identify evidence-based practices for individuals with ASD; and served as project director for the Texas Autism Resource Guide for Teachers (TARGET). Myles is on the executive boards of several organizations, including the Scientific Council of the Organization for Autism Research (SCORE) and ASTEP-Asperger Syndrome Training and Education Program. Further, in the latest survey conducted by the University of Texas, she was acknowledged as the second most productive applied researcher in ASD in the world.

Judy Endow, MSW, is an author and international speaker on a variety of autism-related topics, serves on the Wisconsin DPI Statewide Autism Training Team, and is part of Autistic Global Initiative (AGI). She is a board member of both the Autism Society of America, Wisconsin Chapter, and the Autism National Committee. Endow maintains a private practice in Madison, Wisconsin, providing consultation for families, school districts, and other agencies. Her publications include *Making Lemonade – Hints for Autism's Helpers*, *Paper Words – Discovering and Living with My Autism*, *The Power of Words: How we talk about people with autism spectrum disorders matters!* (DVD), *The Hidden Curriculum Calendar for Older Adolescents and Adults* (2009, 2010), *Outsmarting Explosive Behavior – A Visual System of Support and Intervention for Individuals with Autism Spectrum Disorders*, *Practical Solutions for Stabilizing Students With Classic Autism to Be Ready to Learn: Getting to Go*, and *Learning the*

Hidden Curriculum: The Odyssey of One Autistic Adult. Besides having autism herself, Endow is the parent of three now grown sons, one of whom is on the autism spectrum. In her spare time, Endow enjoys expressing her thoughts and ideas by creating one-of-a-kind hand-built pottery sculptures and painting with acrylics.

Malcolm Mayfield, BS Civil Eng, is a specialist/consultant in Adelaide, Australia, and founder of Autism STAR (autism Spectrum Training, Advocacy & Recruitment), a company that specializes in assisting adults with ASD to be work ready and to integrate into workplaces. His career includes working as a researcher in the UniSA Civil Engineering Laboratories and as a contract administrator in the construction industry. In those capacities, he has worked in teams that have built sports stadiums, high-rise buildings, power stations, and subdivisions, and rose to be highly regarded in his field in the companies for which he worked. His view of the world changed when he self-diagnosed his Asperger Syndrome at the age of 37. Patterns in his life that had previously been confusing at last made sense, and, as part of that process of greater awareness, he realized that in order to cope and succeed as an adult and a professional, he had developed independent success strategies that could be used by others with ASD. Autism STAR grew out of that process of self-discovery. Mayfield's goal is to shine a light on the autism spectrum to show the world that autism is a strength to be cherished and nurtured into success for all.

Advance Praise

"A much-needed, practical and very helpful book targeting an area that is often neglected. Understanding the hidden curriculum within the work and community environment is crucial for our young people, but this book is also useful for employers, coworkers, recruitment consultants, and anybody who is in a position to help somebody with an ASD find suitable employment. Employers will gain a better understanding of the struggles and challenges this population needs to overcome in order to be accepted into society, and in doing so they will learn how they can meet them half-way. Learning the language of ASD can make a big difference for all parties; this books acts as a perfect translation guide."
 – Kevin Baskerville, BEd. [Hons], ACE - Leicestershire, UK Autism outreach service manager & KB Autism Services

"This is an essential, one-of-a-kind guide for any jobseeker or employee on the autism spectrum who may benefit from a black-and-white breakdown of those grey social rules. The book also serves as a useful tool for employers and colleagues of individuals on the autism spectrum, offering unique insight into the perspective of employees who may not understand the hidden curriculum in their workplace. It will be a beneficial resource for AS Capable's clients by providing the tools to confidently navigate the complex social expectations when searching for and maintaining employment."
 – Vicky Little, BA, founder & CEO, AS Capable, North Sydney, Australia

"Members of the autism community are acutely aware of the employment challenges individuals on the autism spectrum face. Many are unemployed, underemployed, and/or live in poverty. *The Hidden Curriculum of Getting and Keeping a Job* is a desperately needed resource to help individuals on the autism spectrum navigate the unwritten rules and expectations of the work environment. This book should be shared with everybody on the spectrum who is pursuing employment or is struggling in their current job. It is one of the most useful books that I have seen in years addressing a growing area of need. Incredible publication. I will recommend it to every professional, family member, and individual who is involved in the employment process."
 – Cathy Pratt, PhD, BCBA-D, Indiana Resource Center for Autism

"As a parent of a daughter with ASD and a professional working in the employment industry, I am very happy to see a book that helps adults with ASD navigate the challenging social landscape of the professional world – from job search, to the interview, to keeping a job. Of particular importance is the section on sexual harassment – both keeping oneself safe and preventing oneself from misunderstandings caused by missing the hidden curriculum. This is an important book for all adults with ASD as well as for teens with ASD planning their post-school careers and their parents."
 – Amanda Tulloch-Hoskins, BA (Hons), Grad. Dip; parent of a 13-year-old girl with ASD; co-creator of iModeling™ (video modeling app) and project manager at Employment Services Company, Adelaide, South Australia

"Finding and keeping a job is difficult for most people but even more so for those with social-cognitive challenges. Brenda Smith Myles, Judy Endow, and Malcolm Mayfield have written a much-needed guide that demystifies this process. Filled with detailed advice and practical rules for approaching the employment world, this book is not only a must-read for individuals who have hidden curriculum challenges, it would also benefit any first-time job seeker looking to improve his or her job search and performance skills."
 – Marcia Scheiner, president, Asperger Syndrome Training & Employment Partnership (ASTEP)

Printed in the USA
CPSIA information can be obtained
at www.ICGtesting.com
JSHW012042140824
68134JS00033B/3203